SARTRE:
LA NAUSÉE and
LES MOUCHES

by

KEITH GORE
Fellow of Worcester College, Oxford

EDWARD ARNOLD

First published 1970 by
Edward Arnold (Publishers) Ltd,
25 Hill Street,
London W1X 8LL

Reprinted 1974
Reprinted with corrections 1977

ISBN: 0 7131 5551 5

Printed in Great Britain by
The Camelot Press Ltd, Southampton

STUDIES IN FRENCH LITERATURE No. 17

General Editor
W. G. Moore
Emeritus Fellow of St John's College, Oxford

Contents

NOTE

The aim of this book is a limited one: that of studying *La Nausée* and *Les Mouches* for themselves and in relation to each other. I shall not, therefore, attempt to view these works within the context of all that Sartre has so far written, nor, with one or two exceptions, make use of his writing since the war; the exceptions are texts (such as *Les Mots*, 1964, or the study of Paul Nizan, 1960) which are, in part, an examination by Sartre of his own attitudes during his earlier years.

The following abbreviations will be used for those texts most frequently quoted: *La Nausée* (*N*), *Les Mouches* (*M*), *Les Mots* (*Mo*). References are to the standard Gallimard editions. I am grateful to Editions Gallimard for permission to quote from Sartre's work.

Introduction

*Le gosse qui rêve d'être champion de boxe, ou
amiral, ou astronaute choisit le réel. Si
l'écrivain choisit l'imaginaire c'est qu'il confond
ces deux domaines.*[1]

There is more than one sense in which Sartre can be called the last
of the pre-war and the first of the post-war writers in France. First, he
may be seen as an author who, mainly thanks to *La Nausée*, emerged
as an important figure in the years immediately prior to 1939, and who,
having had his career interrupted by the war, made a second start after
the Liberation. Such a view is understandable: before 1939, Sartre was
appreciated by a relatively small number of people; after the war, not
only did he make a wider impact through his writing for the theatre,
but he also became a major public figure, thanks to the existentialist
'vogue' of the immediate post-war years. If, however, one looks at
Sartre's career without automatically assuming that the war involved an
interruption in his development, one is led rapidly to the conclusion that
there is in fact a marked continuity in his work. (The point seems fairly
obvious when one considers that *Le Mur*, 1939, was followed by
L'Imaginaire and his first play, *Bariona*, in 1940, *Les Mouches* and *L'Etre
et le néant*—in preparation for some years—in 1943, etc.) Sartre thus
becomes the last of the pre-war and the first of the post-war writers
because he succeeds in bridging the gap of the years 1939–45.

A bridging operation of this kind implies continuity, but also adaptation to a changed situation—and it is here that the bringing together of
La Nausée and *Les Mouches* in a single study is of interest. The Sartre of
the pre-war years was a philosopher by training and by profession, and
not vitally concerned with public affairs: 'apolitique, réfractaire à tout
engagement, j'avais le cœur à gauche, bien sûr, comme chacun';[2] even
the critical year 1933–4, when he was actually in Berlin, did not

---

[1] 'Jean-Paul Sartre s'explique sur *les Mots*', *Le Monde* (samedi 18 avril
1964).

[2] 'Paul Nizan', in *Situations IV* (Paris, Gallimard, 1964), p. 182.

convince him that he should become politically committed. *La Nausée* reflects this situation in that it is philosophical and personal: Roquentin's experience is metaphysical, and concerned with his individual existence. The reassurance he seeks is not through involvement in events and with other men, but by the solitary means of artistic creation—the writing of a novel could bestow on his existence the necessity it does not otherwise seem to possess. In *Les Mouches*, Oreste is aware of a similar problem; the solution he seeks, however, is in marked contrast to that of Roquentin, since he looks to action amongst men as a method of assuring himself of his own necessity.

The continuity from one work to another is shown in the similarity of the preoccupations expressed in them, and these preoccupations, in their turn, echo the ideas expounded in the strictly philosophical works of the pre-war years, as well as in *L'Etre et le néant* of 1943. The contrast results partly from the fact that, whereas in a novel, cast in the form of an intimate diary, it is possible to exploit a personal experience largely to the exclusion of all else, the theatrical tradition within which Sartre works involves showing man *in action* in the world of other men. It arises also, in the case of Sartre, from his evolution away from a personal and theoretical approach to the world towards a view that the individual's existence can have a sense only in terms of a world including other men, and in which action, to be effective, must be undertaken in common with them. *La Nausée* and *Les Mouches*, in other words, when taken together, represent a critical stage in Sartre's development. In an interview given to Jacques-Alain Miller, and published in *L'Express* of 3 March 1960, one finds the following exchange:

> *Sartre:* (. . .) Donc, pas de littérature dégagée, mais profondément dans le monde.
> *Miller:* Pourtant le "Some of these days" de *La Nausée* ressemble fort à la petite phrase de Vinteuil, chez Proust.
> *Sartre:* Cela, c'était tout à fait au début, avant la guerre. J'ai beaucoup évolué depuis. Mes expériences sont devenues de plus en plus sociales à partir de la mobilisation.

What we shall be concerned with is the way in which the change is reflected in our two texts; but we shall be able to do that only if we first of all consider the background out of which *La Nausée* emerges.

*   *   *

This background is closely linked to Sartre's views on the imaginary.

La Nausée itself, of course, as a novel, is a product of the imagination, but it is interesting to find that two of the philosophical works produced by Sartre at the time when he was working on his novel are called *L' Imagination* (published in 1936) and *L'Imaginaire* (published in 1940). And his volume of autobiography, *Les Mots*, not only reveals to us the importance of words in Sartre's life, but also establishes the relationship that exists in his mind between those words and the imaginary world which they can serve to evoke. Let us be clear, however, about what we mean when we use the expression 'imaginary world', if only because, in *L'Imaginaire*, Sartre states 'cette grande loi de l'imagination: *il n'y a pas de monde imaginaire*' (p. 215). A world, he explains, is an organic whole in which each object has its particular place and is related to all the other objects. But the imaginary world is a world of unreal objects, which owe their existence to the person imagining them; consequently, they cannot be in a particular place, since the imagination to which they owe their existence is not physical, and the only relationship they can have is with the imagination on which they depend (p. 170). Sartre by no means denies the *existence* of unreal objects: 'l'objet irréel existe, il existe comme irréel, comme inagissant, sans doute; mais son existence est indéniable' (p. 180). It does not follow that because unreal objects exist, they there-fore exist for us in the same way as real objects; the latter are things which are perceived by us (we *see* the table), whereas unreal objects can be constituted only on the basis of knowledge we already have. This further evidence of their dependence upon us is confirmed by our in-ablity to perceive the time of the unreal world: it has no necessary relationship with time as experienced by us in the real world. The result is that we find ourselves in a curious situation: on the one hand, we may, by the use of our imagination, produce an unreal object; on the other hand, given that we exist in the real world and that the unreal object does not, this product of our imagination must be radically separate from us. Conclusion: 'le monde imaginaire est entièrement isolé, je ne puis y entrer qu'en m'irréalisant' (p. 170). If I want to imagine myself lying in the sun on a South Sea Island beach, I have in a sense to become absent (e.g. from this room in England where I am watching the rain stream down the window) and produce both an imaginary beach and an imaginary self lying on it; this is why someone walking into the room will tell me that I looked as though I was 'miles away'.

The importance of this point is considerable for our purposes. Sartre explains that an imaginary object, although it may be present, is nevertheless beyond our reach—we can neither touch it nor change its position; if we want to throw the imaginary bomb at the imaginary Tsar, we have to become an *imaginary* terrorist to do so. In other words, imaginary objects cannot be acted upon by real people. The fact may not be vital as long as it is no more than a matter of your fantasy world or mine; it takes on a different appearance if the imagination is used to produce a work of art. In this event, the imaginary object, thanks to its expression in the play, the painting, the symphony, the novel, becomes communicable to other people. In the section of *L'Imaginaire* dealing specifically with the work of art (p. 239–46), Sartre takes as his starting-point the notion that 'l'œuvre d'art est un irréel.' Thus, if we can say that a portrait of Charles VIII is an object, we must not lose sight of the fact that it is not the same object as the canvas covered with paint and surrounded with a frame that we hang on the wall. As long as we consider the physical object (canvas, paint, etc.), we shall not see Charles VIII, since they each make their appeal to different forms of our consciousness. Whereas the physical object is accessible to our *conscience réalisante*, we can contemplate 'Charles VIII' only through the operation of the *conscience imageante*, and this involves the suppression of the physical world. Just as it needs an imaginary terrorist to throw an imaginary bomb at an imaginary Tsar, so only a consciousness transposed into the realm of images can contemplate an image of Charles VIII. Consequently, we should take care when talking about the 'real' and the 'imaginary' in art. According to Sartre, it is an error to believe that a painter first of all has an idea in the form of an image which he then realises on his canvas. It may be true that the painter starts off from a mental image which he attempts to communicate to us by painting a picture; it is *not* true that his picture is the image made real, because the real is the paint on the canvas, and no more the image than those other blobs of paint were Charles VIII. What the painter does is to produce what Sartre calls 'un analogon[1] matériel', a physical representation, through the contemplation of which it is possible for us to experience the image the painter wishes to communicate to us. But the image, even when provided with its representation, remains an image. Thus the real painting makes it possible to contemplate an unreal object which I have never seen and never shall see, since it cannot be said to exist *in* the painting, or indeed anywhere in the world; our pleasure does not there-

[1] *Analogon*, that which is analogous; a representation in different circumstances or situation; something performing a corresponding part (*O.E.D.*).

fore come from looking at the paint on the canvas, but from the process by which we apprehend the unreal, imaginary object by means of the physical painting.

In other words, we can say that, in the work of art, the artist creates an unreal object which he communicates to us as an unreal object. And what goes for painting goes, perhaps more obviously, for other forms of art, the novel, poetry, plays. Oliver Twist is not a real person, nor is he simply the printed words we see if we open a copy of *Oliver Twist*; he is an unreal, imaginary character, conveyed to us by Dickens through the use of 'des analoga verbaux', or verbal representation. Similarly, the actor on the stage is not Hamlet, but a man who uses his body, his voice, etc., as an analogon, or physical representation, of the imaginary character created by Shakespeare. Hamlet does not become real in the actor; on the contrary, the actor becomes unreal in order to communicate the unreal character to us: we can begin to 'see' Hamlet only when we stop seeing Laurence Olivier, just as we are unable to 'see' Charles VIII as long as our attention is directed to the paint on the canvas.

But perhaps the most striking example of the unreality of the work of art is to be found in music. When we go to a concert, we go to *hear* a piece of music—say Beethoven's Seventh Symphony. With any luck (if the orchestra does not make too many mistakes, if the conductor does not have a lot of distracting tics, and so on) both orchestra and conductor will efface themselves, and I shall be aware of myself as being in the presence of the Seventh Symphony itself, in person (*en personne*). In what sense, however, can this in fact be so? Clearly, it has nothing to do with the orchestra or the conductor; they are simply performers, and could be replaced by others. Nor has it anything to do with the sound-waves perceived by me, since they are physical phenomena existing in the real world; they are analoga, physical representations which make it possible for me to experience the thing we know as the Seventh Symphony. The Symphony is not on the tip of the conductor's baton, in the instruments, on the pages of the score, or indeed in the concert-hall at all. Like the painting or the novel or the play it is unreal and exists only in the realm of the imaginary; we can be in the presence of the Symphony in person only if we transfer ourselves into the realm of the imaginary —and it is perhaps because it is easier to do this and to avoid the intrusion of the real world that many people close their eyes when listening to music. Consequently, we can say that a piece of music gives itself to us in person at the moment when it is absent from the real listener, and beyond his reach. Here again, the work of art perceived *as* a work of art is something untouchable which cannot be affected by any act of ours.

All the different examples given by Sartre add up to the fact that the work of art exists in a special kind of way. It exists for the artist who creates it; it exists, too, for the person who contemplates the painting, reads the novel, listens to the symphony, etc. But what exists is always an *unreal* object, and that means that, once it has been created, the work of art goes beyond the reach of the artist and his public, and even becomes independent of its physical representation. The artist and his public are real people and can have an effect only on the real world: Beethoven's Seventh Symphony is safe from all of us. If I try to tamper with it, I may produce a bad interpretation of what Beethoven wrote, or perhaps my own First Symphony; but for you, Beethoven's Seventh will remain what it always was. As far as the physical representation (analogon) is concerned, the independence of the work of art follows from the fact that Oliver Twist, for example, is not the book on the shelf. Oliver Twist would not exist for me any the less if all copies of the book were to be destroyed: the destruction of the real books can have no effect on the unreal character. All of which comes down to the idea that the work of art escapes the limitations and the conditions of the real world, for the simple reason that it does not exist in the real world. Once the artist has created it, it exists absolutely and for all time, untouchable and unchangeable.

*　　　*　　　*

The significance of this view of the work of art for Sartre himself quickly becomes apparent. Earlier, in suggesting that the fact of our inability, as real people, to act on imaginary objects was not vital as long as we were concerned only with your fantasy world or mine, we were not saying something which is also true for Sartre. One of his best books, *Les Mots*, is also one which throws a considerable amount of light on his own development, and shows how far the world of fantasy was a major part of his childhood experience. Stated simply, the reason he gives for this fact is that, as a result of his father's death when he himself was a small child, and given his mother's subsequent return to her parents' home, he was put into an abnormal situation in which he had no necessary place. In a sense, he was excluded from the family, since a family consists of parents and a child or children, and in this case, the child was his mother, not him. Moreover, the family represented reality, which meant that, if he was outside the family, he was also outside reality: 'J'étais un faux enfant, je tenais un faux panier à salade; je sentais mes actes se changer en gestes' (*Mo*, p. 67).[1] Obviously, a false child can no more hold a true salad-shaker than a real terrorist can throw an imaginary bomb; and since acts are things which have consequences in the real world, a false child can only be capable of gestures, that is of 'acts' deprived of their consequences (a point which, as we shall see, Oreste fails to grasp). Sartre the small boy, in other words, existed like an imaginary object; while people such as his grandfather seemed to have an absolutely necessary existence in the real world in the sense that it was impossible to conceive of the world without them, Sartre saw himself as supernumerary, someone who would not be missed if he disappeared; someone whose existence in the real world was in no way necessary.

It is not perhaps surprising, therefore, that words should have taken on such an importance for him. In *Les Mots*, he explains how the entries in the *Grand Larousse* appeared to him to represent 'true' men and 'true' animals: 'les gravures, c'étaient leurs corps, le texte, c'était leur âme, leur essence singulière; (. . .) au Jardin d'Acclimatation, les singes étaient moins singes, au Jardin du Luxembourg, les hommes étaient moins hommes' (*Mo*, pp. 38–9). The attitude is highly idealist; every time the pages of the encyclopædia are turned, the pictures appear in exactly the same way as they did the time before, and that is more than can be said for real monkeys or real men. There is a greater inevitability about the men and the monkeys in the encyclopædia than there is about real men and monkeys. Similarly with the accompanying text—and similarly with stories.

Sartre, like all children, was used to hearing his mother tell him stories, but it was a revelation to him when he eventually had books of his own and his mother read to him instead. His explanation of the reason is of considerable interest when one bears in mind his own subsequent career, but also, more immediately for our purposes, in view of the conclusion he provides for *La Nausée*. Here is what he says in *Les Mots*:

> Aux récits improvisés, je vins à préférer les récits préfabriqués; je devins sensible à la succession rigoureuse des mots: à chaque lecture ils revenaient, toujours les mêmes et dans le même ordre, je les attendais. Dans les contes d'Anne-Marie [his mother], les personnages vivaient au petit bonheur, comme elle faisait elle-même: ils acquirent

[1] Jean-Paul Sartre, *Les Mots* (Paris, Gallimard, 1964).

des destins. J'étais à la Messe: j'assistais à l'éternel retour des noms et des événements.

(*Mo*, pp. 35–6)

The stories *told* by his mother were the same, in a general sense, each time of telling—the prince and the princess, one supposes, always lived happily ever after, but the manner of the telling varied with circumstances, depending on the time available, his mother's mood, the degree of Sartre's own attentiveness, and so on. In this respect, they were like the real monkeys and the real men. The inevitability of the men and monkeys in the encyclopædia found its parallel in the *printed* story, where the order of the events, and even of the individual words, was fixed once and for all, and therefore took on an absolute quality. Hence the comparison with the Mass, where the ceremony, the *ritual*, transcends the priest and the congregation, and exists beyond them in an ideal realm. Later on, the impact of the printed story will be confirmed for Sartre in the cinema: there, no matter how many times you see the film, the villain will always succeed in carrying off the young maiden, and the heroine will always succeed in escaping just before the train cuts her in two. But there is an additional element: Sartre knew the cinema before the talkies, and that means that, in his experience, films were closely bound up with music. In the silent cinema, the pianist did not simply accompany the action on the screen, he announced it:

Je me sentais prophète sans rien pouvoir prédire: avant même que le traître eût trahi, son forfait entrait en moi; quand tout semblait tranquille au château, des accords sinistres dénonçaient la présence de l'assassin. Comme ils étaient heureux, ces cow-boys, ces mousquetaires, ces policiers: leur avenir était là, dans cette musique prémonitoire, et gouvernait le présent.

(*Mo*, pp. 101–2)

In the silent cinema, words were more than replaced by music; words can only coincide with the action, whereas music, by its ability to *predict* what is going to happen, imposes upon coming events an absolute character they would not otherwise possess.

One can thus see how the processes of creation through the imagination (words, music, etc.) would appear to Sartre as a means of bringing into the world not only something which existed, but also something which existed in an absolute way *thanks to him*. 'Tout se passa dans ma tête,' he says; 'enfant imaginaire, je me défendis par l'imagination' (*Mo*,

INTRODUCTION   15

p. 92). The imagination made it possible for him to produce works of
the imagination—stories of adventure and the like which would owe
their existence to him, and which, existing, as works of imagination, in
the absolute, would confer upon him the same kind of existence as they
themselves enjoyed: 'Peignant de vrais objets avec de vrais mots tracés
par une vraie plume, ce serait bien le diable si je ne devenais pas vrai
moi aussi' (*Mo*, p. 133). Sartre, the small boy who, in his particular
situation, had the impression that his existence was in no way necessary,
turns to the imaginary and the written work which results from it in
order to confer upon his existence the necessity it otherwise lacks. But
the project is not without its drawbacks:

> L'acte d'imagination (...) est un acte magique. C'est une incantation
> destinée à faire apparaître l'object auquel on pense, la chose qu'on
> désire, de façon qu'on puisse en prendre possession. Il y a, dans cet
> acte, toujours quelque chose d'impérieux et d'enfantin, un refus de
> tenir compte de la distance, des difficultés.
>
> (*L'Imaginaire*, p. 161)

To live through the imagination is a defence against the feeling of being
denied life in the real world; but it is unsatisfactory as a defence in the
sense that it is, in itself, a denial of the real world and involves abandon-
ing the attempt to live in the realm of real people and real objects.
Furthermore, Sartre's boyhood desire to have a *posthumous* reputation as
a famous author is a further example of his attempts to escape from
reality. A posthumous reputation is, by definition, something that the
living author cannot know; consequently, a preoccupation with it can
only be the reflection of a refusal, on the part of the writer, to see his
function as one above all to do with the real world. As time goes on and
Sartre becomes more concerned with the idea of commitment in literature, he will move away from that standpoint and towards the view that
the writer has a positive role to play in the here and now, and should
produce his work against the background of the concrete problems of
the world around him. But the process will be a long one. He himself
situates in about 1954 the moment at which he finally realised that the
individual cannot achieve salvation through literature—that is to say
through works of the imagination. This is how he puts the point in an
interview published by *Le Monde* in April 1964:

> Il n'y a de salut nulle part. L'idée de salut implique l'idée d'un absolu.
> Pendant quarante ans j'ai été mobilisé par l'absolu, la névrose. L'absolu

est parti. Restent des tâches, innombrables, parmi lesquelles la littéra-
ture n'est aucunement privilégiée.

That stage in his development is not reached, however, until relatively
late in his career. *La Nausée* and *Les Mouches* both represent steps in the
evolution which leads up to it.

La Nausée

En face d'un enfant qui meurt, la Nausée *ne fait pas le poids.*[1]

In a sense, *La Nausée* is a very simple novel: it begins with the realisation by Roquentin that the relationship between him and the objects around him is a disturbing one, and ends with the discovery of a possible solution in the realm of the imaginary, since that realm is radically independent of the physical world. The working-out of the solution is not so simple, and leads us through the discussion of a number of themes, all of which are more or less directly related to the questions we examined in our Introduction. As far as Sartre's own preoccupations are concerned, he himself establishes the link with his novel:

> Je réussis à trente ans ce beau coup: d'écrire dans *La Nausée*—bien sincèrement, on peut me croire—l'existence injustifiée, saumâtre de mes congénères et mettre la mienne hors de cause. *J'étais* Roquentin, je montrais en lui, sans complaisance, la trame de ma vie; en même temps j'étais *moi*, l'élu, annaliste des enfers, photomicroscope de verre et d'acier penché sur mes propres sirops protoplasmiques.
>
> (*Mo*, pp. 209–10)

Our analysis of *La Nausée* will therefore echo this parallel, and will also be an attempt to isolate the other major themes, to show how they are related to each other, and make clear how they all, in their various ways, contribute to make it possible for Roquentin finally to come to a conclusion about his relationship with the world around him.

One of the things that a careful reading of *La Nausée* brings out with some force is the fact that the various elements in the novel all play their part in helping Roquentin to understand the nature of his initial experience: it is indeed true that scenes like the description of the rue Tournebride on a Sunday morning, the visit to the portrait gallery, the reunion with Anny, or the Autodidacte's disgrace are all set pieces;

[1] 'Jean-Paul Sartre s'explique sur *les Mots*', *op. cit.*

nevertheless, each of them helps to throw light upon the state of Roquentin's thinking at the moment when they take place, and also points the
way forward to a closer understanding of the situation in which he finds
himself. This, after all, is hardly surprising. The very first entry in
Roquentin's diary (the *feuillet sans date*) begins with these words: 'Le
mieux serait d'écrire les événements au jour le jour. Tenir un journal
pour y voir clair. Ne pas laisser échapper les nuances, les petits faits,
même s'ils n'ont l'air de rien, et surtout les classer' (*N*, p. 11).[1] It is not
simply a matter of recording facts, for, as Roquentin explains, his aim is
to describe *how* he perceives the world around him—he is looking for
explanations, and will therefore reflect upon the experiences he under-
goes. If, therefore, he notes in his diary: 'Rien. Existé' (*N*, p. 133), we
should not assume that nothing in particular happened on the Tuesday
in question, but that the two-word entry represents its writer's state of
mind on that particular day. Our task will consist in following the
processes of Roquentin's thought, interpreting them as we go, in order
that we may evaluate the significance of the different entries at the point
where they occur in the diary.

Such a method does not imply that we should concern ourselves too
much with the way in which the novel is presented to us. The 'Avertisse-
ment des éditeurs', the footnotes in the first few pages, are purely
conventional, and do not mean that we are to be very interested in the
fact that the Autodidacte was called Ogier P . . . , or even to worry
about the reasons *why* Roquentin's manuscript should have been found
by someone among his papers: there is no reason to suppose that Roquentin went mad or committed suicide; and even if he had, it would not be
of any significance for the understanding of the novel, since the book
itself leads neither towards madness nor towards suicide, and they would
therefore have to be explained by causes alien to the novel.

For the greater part of its length, *La Nausée* provides an account of
events as they are experienced by Roquentin; although he can obviously
write up his diary only after having gone through the experiences he
recounts, his desire to transcribe these experiences as directly as possible
results in a narration which is often in the present tense, and which in
any case gives an impression of immediacy. This is not true, however, of
the first entry in the diary; the *feuillet sans date* expresses the intention to
note things *as* they happen, but is in itself an attempt to interpret what
has already been experienced: 'Ce qui s'est passé en moi n'a pas laissé

[1] Jean-Paul Sartre, *La Nausée* (Paris, Gallimard, 1938).

de traces claires. Il y avait quelque chose que j'ai vu et qui m'a dégoûté, mais je ne sais plus si je regardais la mer ou le galet' (N, p. 12). The use of the conjunction *mais* serves to underline the lack of relationship between the disgust and the act of looking. Only when the diary proper begins does Roquentin in fact begin to keep an 'objective' record. The distinction between recording and interpreting is well shown in a passage in which he remarks on the difference between events as he observes them and as they are told by the sort of men he sees in cafés. First of all, there is the 'objective' description:

> samedi, vers quatre heures de l'après-midi, sur le bout de trottoir en planches du chantier de la gare, une petite femme en bleu ciel courait à reculons, en riant, en agitant un mouchoir. En même temps, un nègre avec un imperméable crème, des chaussures jaunes et un chapeau vert, tournait le coin de la rue et sifflait. La femme est venue le heurter, toujours à reculons, sous une lanterne qui est suspendue à la palissade et qu'on allume le soir.

Then comes the 'interpretation':

> A quatre ou cinq, je suppose que nous aurions remarqué le choc, toutes ces couleurs tendres, le beau manteau bleu qui avait l'air d'un édredon, l'imperméable clair, les carreaux rouges de la lanterne; nous aurions ri de la stupéfaction qui paraissait sur ces deux visages d'enfants.

The episode serves to give some indication of the reason for Roquentin's experience of nausea. Normally, our approach towards things is conditioned by the fact that we integrate them into the totality of our *human* experience; a woman bumping into a negro is not a series of unrelated actions, but an organic episode which is, for example, comic, because we see it and comprehend it in human terms: the surprise of the woman, the negro's attempts to avoid the collision, etc. Since Roquentin lives in a state of solitude, events and objects have tended to become divorced from their human connotations; events disintegrate as soon as they are complete because they do not become part of a complex of references, as when the story is told by one man to another:

> Puis (l'ensemble) s'est disloqué, il n'est resté que la lanterne, la palissade et le ciel: c'était encore assez beau. Une heure après, la lanterne était allumée, le vent soufflait, le ciel était noir: il ne restait plus rien du tout.

(N, pp. 19–20.)

Applied to objects, this fact takes on more dramatic significance; if objects cease to be perceived in some kind of relationship to man, Roquentin discovers, they can begin to impose themselves upon him as objects independent of the meaning we normally give them. A doorknob is a door-knob, that is to say a metal object made by men so that men may achieve given aims (passing from one room to another, and so on). Freed from its subservience to the needs of men, it takes on a different kind of existence:

> Les objets, cela ne devrait pas *toucher*, puisque cela ne vit pas. On s'en sert, on les remet en place, on vit au milieu d'eux: ils sont utiles, rien de plus. Et moi, ils me touchent, c'est insupportable. J'ai peur d'entrer en contact avec eux tout comme s'ils étaient des bêtes vivantes.

This is the origin of Roquentin's nausea. In the *feuillet sans date*, where he first mentions the famous pebble he was incapable of keeping in his hand, he can offer no explanation for what he felt. Once he is aware of objects as having 'une sorte de personnalité' (N, p. 15), he can be a little more precise about his reaction:

> Maintenant, je vois; je me rappelle mieux ce que j'ai senti, l'autre jour, au bord de la mer, quand je tenais ce galet. C'était une espèce d'écœurement douceâtre. Que c'était donc désagréable! Et cela venait du galet, j'en suis sur, cela passait du galet dans mes mains. Oui, c'est cela, c'est bien cela: une sorte de nausée dans les mains.
>
> (N, p. 23)

The physical contact with an object outside himself has provoked a feeling of 'localised' nausea at the point of contact—his hands. But the important thing is that the nausea does not originate in the Roquentin of whom the hands are a part, but seems rather to have come from the pebble. The pebble *touches him*, and also transmits the nausea into his hands: clearly the experience of nausea is a result of the breakdown of the customary relationship between Roquentin and the world of objects. And those objects need not be outside himself, as is apparent when he stares at himself in the mirror, and sees his own face as an object:

> Je n'y comprends rien, à ce visage. Ceux des autres ont un sens. Pas le mien. Je ne peux même pas décider s'il est beau ou laid. Je pense qu'il est laid, parce qu'on me l'a dit. Mais cela ne me frappe pas. Au fond je suis même choqué qu'on puisse lui attribuer des qualités de ce genre, comme si on appelait beau ou laid un morceau de terre ou bien un bloc de rocher.
>
> (N, p. 30)

The qualities of beauty or ugliness, of course, make sense only in human terms, just as other mens' faces have a meaning because we see in them more than simply their external, physical characteristics. *Your* face means something to me because it expresses you as a human being; *my* face means something to me because it is what other people recognise me by—and I am not simply the physical me. Roquentin, however, lives in isolation from other men, and his face is no more than an assemblage of pores, hairs, veins, and so on:

> Les yeux, le nez et la bouche disparaissent: il ne reste plus rien d'humain. Des rides brunes de chaque côté du gonflement fiévreux des lèvres, des crevasses, des taupinières. Un soyeux duvet blanc court sur les grandes pentes des joues, deux poils sortent des narines: c'est une carte géologique en relief.
>
> (*N*, p. 31)

The first twenty pages of the novel thus reveal to us not only that Roquentin's nausea arises from his relationship with the objects in the world around him, but also from his situation with regard to other men. Our knowledge of his plight will be considerably extended during the first 'set-piece' description of his nausea during the scene at the café 'Le Rendez-vous des Cheminots', although it is true that he does not experience it in exactly the same way as when he picked up the pebble on the sea-shore. This time, nausea is associated with the various sense impressions which come to him from the room around him: colours, sounds, movements. Adolphe's braces are seen as a mauve patch on the background of his shirt; the shirt is a blue patch against the chocolate-coloured wall; the wall delimits the environment in which Roquentin finds himself, and it is because it now comes from the whole of his physical surroundings rather than from one object that the feeling of nausea is no longer localised but something which encloses him: 'La Nausée n'est pas en moi: je la ressens *là-bas* sur le mur, sur les bretelles, partout autour de moi. Elle ne fait qu'un avec le café, c'est moi qui suis en elle' (*N*, p. 34). In fact, however, Roquentin does not remain totally submerged in this nausea; unable any longer to bear the sight of Adolphe swaying backwards and forwards behind the bar, he asks the waitress to put on his favourite record, which will be of great importance in the later part of the novel: *Some of these days*. As soon as the music starts, it begins to have its effect on Roquentin—and in writing of it, he uses expressions strikingly similar to those to be found in *Les Mots* when Sartre describes his childhood reaction to stories and to the cinema:

Pour l'instant, c'est le jazz qui joue; il n'y a pas de mélodie, juste des notes, une myriade de petites secousses. Elles ne connaissent pas de repos, un ordre inflexible les fait naître et les détruit, sans leur laisser jamais le loisir de se reprendre, d'exister pour soi.

(N, p. 36)

It is precisely the *ordre inflexible*, which goes beyond the actual sounds he hears, that acts upon Roquentin: 'Je commence à me réchauffer, à me sentir heureux.' The music can have this result because it exists in such a radically different way from the world of objects which produces nausea in him, and yet, curiously, Roquentin describes it in terms which make it seem more consistent than the objects of the material world: the music is a *ruban d'acier*, unaffected by the vet and his daughter when they come into the café: 'la musique perce ces formes vagues et passe au travers.' Roquentin does not concern himself with the reason why the physical world should be thus reduced in status, except insofar as he notes that it is inseparable from time ('ce temps ou le monde est affalé'—N, p. 37). Although the record revolves in a world governed by time, the music remains independent of that world, and the song of the negress, since it is part of the music, is bound to come: 'Ça semble inévitable, si forte est la nécessité de cette musique'. Naturally, Roquentin can hear the sounds only in the world of time—he is part of that world, and must wait the length of time needed for the needle to move across the record to the point at which the sounds will be reproduced. But the song itself *does not* have to 'wait' until a given amount of time has elapsed; it makes itself heard because it is part of a fixed sequence of sounds and cannot help taking its place in that sequence. When we go to the cinema, we know that the hero will rescue the heroine from the oncoming train *because the director has arranged things that way*, and not for any reasons to do with time: the sequence will remain the same at whatever time of the day you see it, or indeed at whatever speed the film is put through the projector. Roquentin is attached to *Some of these days* because of its inevitability, because he knows that, once the first note has been heard, the refrain must follow. And as he listens to the negress singing, his nausea suddenly disappears. When he was completely in the grip of nausea, he wrote 'c'est moi qui suis en elle'; now, he notes: 'Je suis *dans* la musique.' The nausea disappears as he ceases to become aware of the world of objects and becomes absorbed into the realm of music; in other words, nausea is associated not only with the relationship between Roquentin and the physical world, but also with a difference in nature between the exist-

ence of that world and of music. What that difference is he will understand more clearly as time goes on.

Meanwhile, his diary sets off on a new tack, apparently more to do
with people than with things. As his examination of his own face in the
mirror showed, Roquentin is aware that people also belong to the world
of objects; the next section of *La Nausée* is in many ways a reflection
upon that awareness. It is worth noting that this new stage in the development of the novel starts off in a way similar to that adopted to underline
the difference we observed between 'objective' description and 'interpretation', although this time the juxtaposition is not as evident as in the
previous case. An earlier entry in the diary had recounted the suffering of
Lucie, chamber-maid at Roquentin's hotel. Her unhappiness comes
from the fact that her handsome young husband is going to the bad, not
so much through womanising as through drink and ill-health. But
Roquentin has the impression that she is not authentic in her suffering:

> Elle souffre en avare. Elle doit être avare aussi pour ses plaisirs. Je me
> demande si elle ne souhaite pas, quelquefois, d'être délivrée de cette
> douleur monotone, de ces marmonnements qui reprennent dès
> qu'elle ne chante plus, si elle ne souhaite pas de souffrir un bon coup,
> de se noyer dans le désespoir.
>
> (*N*, p. 24)

Normally, then, she 'organises' her suffering, makes it correspond to
some idea she has of what is appropriate. Things are different when,
having listened to *Some of these days*, Roquentin leaves the café and walks
along the boulevard Noir. In his state of freedom from nausea, he is
above all sensitive to the boulevard as a kind of no-man's-land: 'On
n'habite pas cette région du boulevard Noir' (*N*, p. 40). It somehow escapes from the normal categories because, although it obviously belongs
to the world of physical existants, and owes its form to men, it is nevertheless, in its abandonment, independent of both, and consequently has
an existence similar to that of a piece of music: 'je suis gagné par la
pureté de ce qui m'entoure; rien ne vit; le vent siffle, des lignes raides
fuient dans la nuit. Le boulevard Noir n'a pas la mine indécente des
rues bourgeoises, qui font des grâces aux passants' (*N*, p. 41). Later, he
adds: 'Le boulevard Noir est inhumain. Comme un minéral. Comme un
triangle.' And like, one might add, *Some of these days*. Walking along the
boulevard, happy in his freedom from nausea, and wishing that he could
participate in the particular 'purity' of his surroundings, he notices two

people, Lucie and her husband, arguing. As he draws nearer, the man pushes the woman away, and leaves her. Roquentin is amazed by the difference in Lucie. He recognises her, but only in physical terms:

> Oui, c'est elle, c'est Lucie. Mais transfigurée, hors d'elle-même, souffrant avec une folle générosité. (. . .) Mais elle ne bouge pas, elle a l'air minéralisée comme tout ce qui l'entoure. Un instant je me demande si je ne m'étais pas trompé sur elle, si ce n'est pas sa vraie nature qui m'est soudain révélée . . .
>
> (N, p. 43)

By becoming submerged in her suffering, Lucie has freed herself from her everyday practical and 'positive' existence, and has escaped into a realm where she is so far removed from reality that she does not even recognise Roquentin when she looks at him. Lucie takes on the appearance of a mineral, just as *Some of these days* was like a strip of steel, just as the sound of a bell had seemed to Roquentin 'harder' and less 'human' than other, more domesticated, noises.

We may say, therefore, that the difference between material objects and a piece of music has a parallel in the difference between people in their ordinary experience of everyday life, and people in those moments when they forget themselves and allow themselves to be carried away by, for example, pure suffering. When Roquentin looks out of the library window and sees women walking their dogs round the statue of Gustave Impétraz, he recognises them as the same kind of people as Lucie; like her, they live according to conventional norms of behaviour, feeling, and so on, with the result that they see in the statue, not a work of art, but the reassuring figure of a man who guarantees that they are right to live in such a way: 'les saintes idées, les bonnes idées qu'elles tiennent de leurs pères, elles n'ont plus la responsabilité de les défendre; un homme de bronze s'en est fait le gardien' (N, p. 44). Similarly with the Autodidacte, whose ambition to read all the books in the public library from A to Z stems from his exaggerated respect for the human knowledge and values perpetuated by the printed word, and incarnated in people like Gustave Impétraz.

Such confidence, as we shall see, is misplaced; nevertheless, the fact is that the old women, like the Autodidacte, are in this respect characteristic of a more widespread human tendency, the desire to see life in general, and one's own life in particular, as being predictable, and somehow destined to follow a certain course. Roquentin himself is not free from this tendency, and his preoccupation with the theme of Adventure shows this. Looking out of another window, this time in his hotel room, he becomes fascinated by the movements of an old woman in the street below. He can *see* which way she is heading, he *knows* that after a certain time she will turn the corner and disappear from sight: 'Je *vois* l'avenir. Il est là, posé dans la rue, à peine plus pâle que le présent. Qu'a-t-il besoin de se réaliser? Qu'est-ce que ça lui donnera de plus?' (*N*, p. 47). The point comes at which he can no longer be sure whether he is observing the woman's movements or foreseeing them; present and future lose their separate identity: 'C'est ça le temps, le temps tout nu, ça vient lentement à l'existence, ça se fait attendre et quand ça vient, on est écœuré parce qu'on s'aperçoit que c'était déjà là depuis longtemps' (*N*, p. 48). This is undoubtedly true; we may often be unable to foretell the outcome of a given event, but once the event is complete, its outcome is so much a part of it that it takes on an appearance of complete inevitability, and in this sense was 'déjà là depuis longtemps'. Once the event has happened, it no longer has anything to do with the present or the future, but only with the past, with history. Roquentin realises this more clearly when, having succeeded in dragging himself away from the window, he lies down on his bed and tries to evoke images from his past life. He has discovered that, with the passage of time, such images have become more and more difficult to call up. What he often finds is that *images* tend to be replaced by *memories*; both the Arab who attacked him in Meknès and the doctor he knew in Baku were blind in one eye. When he tries to recall either of them, what he sees is the blind eye. Is it the blind eye of the right man, however? And does he *see* it? Faced with this uncertainty, he can no longer be sure that even such fragmentary evocations are memories, or merely inventions: 'Il y a beaucoup de cas d'ailleurs où ces bribes elles-mêmes ont disparu: il ne reste plus que des mots' (*N*, p. 49). The memories and the images were *his* past, and as long as he could recall them in their totality, their link with him seemed still to exist; the present Roquentin could be identified with Roquentin in the past. But once the memories lose their immediacy and become intellectualised in the form of words, they escape from him. He exists in the present; an event evoked through words does not exist in the world of material time any more than a piece of music does. Therefore Roquentin, cut off from his past, becomes a prisoner in the present:

Jamais je n'ai eu si fort qu'aujourd'hui le sentiment d'être sans dimensions secrètes, limité à mon corps, aux pensées légères qui

montent de lui commes des bulles. Je construis mes souvenirs avec
mon présent. Je suis rejeté, délaissé dans le présent. Le passé, j'essaie en
vain de le rejoindre: je ne peux pas m'échapper.

(*N*, p. 50)

How far the events of Roquentin's past life have become detached
from him is made clear with the arrival of the Autodidacte, who has
come to see his collection of photographs and picture post-cards, the
pictorial representation, for him, of places where adventures come
about. He assumes that, since Roquentin has been to these places, he
must have had adventures; Roquentin, up to now, has made the same
assumption himself. All of a sudden, he has doubts: 'il me semble que je
mens, que de ma vie je n'ai eu la moindre aventure, ou plutôt je ne sais
même plus ce que ce mot veut dire' (*N*, p. 53). Once he has got rid of
the Autodidacte, he is free to examine the reasons for his doubts, and
quickly comes to the conclusion that what he has taken for adventures
were no more than events or incidents which had happened to him.
Adventures do not happen in real life; they can only exist as stories:
'Les aventures sont dans les livres. Et naturellement, tout ce qu'on
raconte dans les livres peut arriver pour de vrai, mais pas de la même
manière. C'est à cette manière d'arriver que je tenais si fort' (*N*, p. 55).
Roquentin's mistake, then, was to seek in the events of his life the formal
completeness of the stories that people tell or write down in books. The
assumption he made was that our experience builds itself up in identi-
fiable, autonomous sections, whereas in fact our life is a continuous flow,
in which one moment merges into another, and in which *while we are
living it* no event has a formal beginning or end. It is only in retrospect
that we can see it as a whole and transform a lived event into an Adventure: 'Je me retourne; derrière moi, cette belle forme mélodique
s'enfonce tout entière dans le passé. Elle diminue, en déclinant elle se
contracte, à présent la fin ne fait plus qu'un avec le commencement' (*N*,
p. 56). Consequently, we can make the most banal event into an adventure by the simple process of recounting it. And indeed, for
Roquentin, this is what most people do; on the one hand, they spend a
lot of time in recounting their life as a series of stories; on the other
hand, they attempt to live their life as though it is a story being told by
them. 'Mais il faut choisir: vivre ou raconter' (*N*, p. 57). Living is a
matter of undergoing a number of experiences which follow each other
more or less haphazardly and take on an overall sense only in retrospect;
to suppose that one's life is like a story is to assume that the end already

exists, and that, therefore, the events of one's life are in some way predetermined. 'J'ai voulu', writes Roquentin, 'que les moments de ma vie
se suivent et s'ordonnent comme ceux d'une vie qu'on se rappelle.
Autant vaudrait tenter d'attraper le temps par la queue' (N, p. 59).

Roquentin, largely no doubt because of his isolation from other people
and the consequent lack of incident in his life, has understood that life
cannot be lived in this way; the inhabitants of Bouville are excellent
examples of people who have not. The way in which, during the Sunday
morning parade up and down the rue Tournebride, each accepts himself
as occupying a fixed place in the social hierarchy is evidence of this fact.
Their situation in the hierarchy defines them in terms of other people;
the function that goes with that place determines the role they must
play—in other words, the course of their life is indeed predetermined, it
is a story told in advance, the present is conditioned by the future. Time
is reversed: instead of moving out of their past towards their future,
they are in the position of seeing their future (the end of their story)
dictate their past and their present existence.

We are shown how impossible this process is in terms of actual
living through Roquentin's experience at the end of the Sunday in
question. All of a sudden, he has the feeling that he is going to have an
adventure. As he walks, he tells himself that something will happen when
he reaches a certain point; when nothing in fact happens, he decides that
the point must be further on, and finally concludes, when he is in front
of the café Mably, that what he had been heading towards was the sight
of the cashier seated behind the till inside the café. The facts in themselves
are of the utmost banality and, looking back, Roquentin rightly concludes that the feeling of adventure does not come from them but rather
from a consciousness of the flow of time: 'brusquement on sent que le
temps s'écoule, que chaque instant conduit à un autre instant, celui-ci
à un autre et ainsi de suite' (N, p. 77). One becomes aware of being
carried by time into the future, of going forward towards something, of
acting in such a way that one commits the future, without knowing
what the future will be. Time, in this situation, is not reversed; on the
contrary: 'Le sentiment de l'aventure serait, tout simplement, celui de
l'irréversibilité du temps' (N, p. 78). Roquentin's former mistress, Anny,
was not above trying to manipulate time to produce a feeling of this
kind. He tells us that when he used to travel from Aden to Djibouti to
spend twenty-four hours with her, she would make sure that they remained at loggerheads until only one hour was left: 'soixante minutes,

juste le temps qu'il faut pour qu'on sente passer les secondes une à une'
(N, p. 78). The knowledge that they must separate in an hour itself
produced an impression of the irreversibility of time and an acute awareness of its flow. But, for Anny, it was not so much a matter of trying to
experience an impression of adventure as a desire to create *moments
parfaits*.

Adventures, it will be remembered, can only be *stories*, and so must
be divorced from the real world. Perfection being an abstract quality,
the perfect moments which Anny attempts to realise must exist on the
same level as adventures. What Roquentin tells us about them bears this
out. A story is something which, once it is told or written down, exists
independently of the teller or the writer. In this respect, it is like a piece
of music, whose notes follow one another in a fixed succession. Another
human activity shares the same characteristic: ritual, in which gestures
are made and words spoken according to an inflexible order. The form
of the ritual is independent of the people who perform it. Anny's ambition to realise perfect moments showed itself in the attempt to transform her life into ritual, but since ritual is outside time and beyond
reality, whilst we live in a real world governed by time, she could have
no hope of success: 'je me débattais', writes Roquentin, 'au milieu de
rites qu'Anny inventait sur le moment et je les déchirais de mes grands
bras comme des toiles d'araignée. A ces moments-là elle me haïssait'
(N, p. 85). She was less than fair, not only because Roquentin, a real man,
could not know the idea present to her mind, but also because it is
impossible, given the abstract nature of ritual, to create it out of experience which is in the process of being lived. Roquentin will respond
to her summons to go and see her in Paris, because, he says, he is still in
love with her, but also partly, no doubt, to discover whether her attitude
to perfect moments has changed.

Meanwhile, he is brought back to his reflections upon the other people
he sees about him in Bouville. His examination of the society of the
town had begun with the statue of Impétraz, and continued with his
observation of the bourgeois during their Sunday morning walk in the
rue Tournebride. It is carried a stage further with the entry into the
restaurant 'chez Camille', where Roquentin is having lunch, of Dr Rogé,
a man confident of his place in the world: 'Voilà ce que j'appelle une
belle tête d'homme. Usée, creusée par la vie et les passions. Mais le docteur
a compris la vie, dominé ses passions' (N, p. 89). His self-assurance is
so great that he is able to give reassurance to others, but always, it

should be added, on the basis of his own superiority. He is the sort of man who, because he has 'lived' and knows what suffering is, believes that he possesses an accumulation of Experience which he can now put at the disposal of others. What it means is that he uses his *past* to govern the *present* of those about him; the actual process of living can no longer exist because, instead of moving forward into the future, people like Dr Rogé remain perpetually turned towards reference points in the past:

> Ils voudraient nous faire croire que leur passé n'est pas perdu, que leurs souvenirs se sont condensés, moelleusement convertis en Sagesse. Commode passé! Passé de poche, petit livre doré plein de belles maximes. "Croyez-moi, je vous parle d'expérience, tout ce que je sais, je le tiens de la vie." Est-ce que la Vie se serait chargée de penser pour eux? Ils expliquent le neuf par l'ancien—et l'ancien, ils l'ont expliqué par des événements plus anciens encore, comme ces historiens qui font de Lénine un Robespierre russe et de Robespierre un Cromwell français: au bout du compte, ils n'ont jamais rien compris du tout . . .

(N, p. 92)

Their experience of life is, in practice, a means whereby they can avoid actually having to live, and involves the assumption that the world about them is unchanging and can be counted upon to remain so.

This assumption can be made only if it is universally accepted. Roquentin, living alone, rather than surrounded by other men, is not certain that it can be made, especially when he finds himself in a town transformed by fog. In the earlier stages of his diary he had written: 'dans les cafés, tout est toujours normal et particulièrement au café Mably, à cause du gérant, M. Fasquelle, qui porte sur sa figure un air de canaillerie bien positif et rassurant' (*N*, p. 18). He is therefore particularly disturbed when, on the foggy morning, he goes to the 'café Mably' for breakfast, only to find it almost deserted and devoid of the reassuring presence of the *patron*, who, contrary to his habit, has not come down from his flat. Roquentin imagines that M. Fasquelle might be dead, but he is less concerned by that possibility than by the fact that the failure to conform to custom somehow brings into question the existence of things in general: 'C'est par paresse, je suppose, que le monde se ressemble d'un jour à l'autre. Aujourd'hui, il avait l'air de vouloir changer. Et alors *tout, tout* pouvait arriver' (*N*, p. 102). If Roquentin can only see M. Fasquelle again he will once more be reassured; but when he returns to the 'café Mably', he finds it completely deserted. He is seized by panic at this discovery: M. Fasquelle is not as reassuring as he appeared; perhaps nothing is what it seems. How does he know that things do not become different when his back is turned? Perhaps he can be sure that they will retain their identity only if he keeps his eyes fixed on them and repeats their names to himself: 'je me disais avec force: c'est un bec de gaz, c'est une borne-fontaine et j'essayais, par la puissance de mon regard, de les réduire à leur aspect quotidien' (*N*, p. 103). But even the process of applying to things the names by which we identify them does not guarantee their docility—we have no proof that the world is as tame as we think it is.

Or more precisely as we claim to think it is. Roquentin is not alone in being aware that the world does not necessarily have to exist in the well-ordered, conventional way to which we are accustomed, or in knowing that we ourselves do not occupy a necessary place in a fixed system organised around us. This is why people like Dr Rogé give such pride of place to experience: 'c'est leur dernière défense. Le docteur voudrait bien y croire, il voudrait se masquer l'insoutenable réalité: qu'il est seul, sans acquis, sans passé, avec une intelligence qui s'empâte, un corps qui se défait' (*N*, p. 93). What is perhaps the most brilliant scene in *La Nausée*—Roquentin's visit to the portrait gallery at the museum— provides further illustration of this point. Significantly, he goes to the museum because he is puzzled by the physical proportions of the portrait of Olivier Blévigne. He discovers that Blévigne was in fact a very small man, but that the portraitist had painted his picture in such a way that the subject seemed to be of normal size: 'Admirable puissance de l'art. De ce petit homme à la voix suraiguë, rien ne passerait à la postérité, qu'une face menaçante, qu'un geste superbe et des yeux sanglants de taureau' (*N*, p. 121). Olivier Blévigne as appearance and as reality is two different things. In this respect, he is like all the other citizens of Bouville portrayed in the gallery: each of them was a man like any other, but each played out the part of someone who, unlike others, was an essential element in society, whose role bestowed upon his existence some absolute necessity: Pacôme, whose attention to his duty had given him the right to exist; the grandfather, whose name was unimportant—he incarnated Experience: 'Je n'avais pas été assez loin l'autre jour: l'Expérience était bien plus qu'une défense contre la mort; elle était un droit: le droit des vieillards' (*N*, p. 113); Parrotin, the doctor who 'understood' everyone, even revolutionaries, and knew how to direct them back into the path of duty; Olivier Blévigne himself, who, despite his lack of height, knew both his duties and his rights. Faced with such a series of solid bourgeois, Roquentin might be tempted to doubt his right to exist. He knows, however, thanks to the trick employed in the portrayal of Olivier Blévigne, that the portraits do no more than perpetuate the vision that their subjects wished others to have of them. They wanted to be seen as different from other men: if they are *salauds*, it is because they are guilty of that *mauvaise foi* that Sartre will analyse in detail in later works, it is because their desire to seem different involves hiding both from themselves and from others that their existence is no more necessary than anyone else's.

The visit to the portrait gallery is not unrelated to Roquentin's decision to abandon his biography of the marquis de Rollebon: 'Comment donc', he asks himself, 'moi qui n'ai pas eu la force de retenir mon propre passé, puis-je espérer que je sauverai celui d'un autre?' (N, p. 123). He realises that he who, as a man, has no necessary existence, cannot bestow necessary existence upon Rollebon. The very act of writing the biography proves it: the paper on which he writes exists in the present; so do the words he has written—as the ink dries, they not only become part of the material world, which *always* exists in the present, but also separate themselves from him. All of a sudden, he realises a fact which has so far escaped him: 'La vraie nature du présent se dévoilait: il était ce qui existe, et tout ce qui n'était pas présent n'existait pas' (N, p. 124). The only things that exist, in other words, are material things. Roquentin himself, therefore, can exist only in physical terms; but none of us exists merely as a body: when I say 'I', the reference is normally to my mind rather than to my body. As Sartre says elsewhere: 'La conscience et le monde sont donnés d'un même coup: extérieur par essence à la conscience, le monde est, par essence, relatif à elle'.[1]

Mind takes precedence over body, therefore, but we are nevertheless aware of existing both as mind and as body. It is at the point where Roquentin becomes conscious that we exist on these two levels that he finds himself once again gripped by the experience of nausea. Not, perhaps, surprisingly: the long section of the diary which has been centred mainly on other people as a subject for reflection has led him back to the question of the existence of the material world and to the problem of the relationship between himself and that material world. On this occasion, the attack of nausea is particularly violent. All that he has written on the subject of adventure, perfect moments, time,

[1] 'Une idée fondamentale de Husserl', *Situations I* (Paris, 1947), p. 32.

salauds, and so on, has been a preparation for the realisation that, having dropped his book on Rollebon—up to now a justification for his existence—he is alone, face to face with the world of objects and thus a prisoner of the present, but knowing that he can no more find any necessity for his existence in the present than in the past or the future. 'M. de Rollebon était mon associé: il avait besoin de moi pour être et j'avais besoin de lui pour ne pas sentir mon être' (*N*, p. 127): this sentence introduces a passage which reaches the level of delirium as Roquentin attempts to make clear to himself exactly what should be understood when we speak of 'being'. The actual experience of nausea has always been provoked by the perception (touch, vision, etc.) of objects. On this new occasion, the experience takes a different form: 'La chose, qui attendait, s'est alertée, elle a fondu sur moi, elle se coule en moi, j'en suis plein. — Ce n'est rien: la Chose, c'est moi. L'existence, libérée, dégagée, reflue sur moi. J'existe' (*N*, p. 127). When he picked up the pebble, nausea came from the awareness of the effect of the pebble as object upon Roquentin as consciousness; when it came from the total environment of the cafe, it was again because of Roquentin's perception of his surroundings in terms of the material world. The difference now is that the object which causes nausea is *Roquentin himself,* so that when he says 'J'existe', the 'I' refers to his body and is no longer the 'I' of consciousness or mind:

> Je vois ma main, qui s'épanouit sur la table. Elle vit—c'est moi. Elle s'ouvre, les doigts se déploient et pointent. Elle est sur le dos. Elle me montre son ventre gras. Elle a l'air d'une bête à la renverse. Les doigts, ce sont les pattes. (. . .) Je sens ma main. C'est moi, ces deux bêtes qui s'agitent au bout de mes bras.
>
> (*N*, pp. 127–8)

The hand both *is* Roquentin as body and *is not* Roquentin as mind, and he can do nothing about the fact, since the body is something for whose existence he is not initially responsible: as far as he is concerned, it is simply there. The same cannot be said of his thoughts: 'Le corps, ça vit tout seul, une fois que ça a commencé. Mais la pensée, c'est *moi* qui la continue, qui la déroule. J'existe. Je pense que j'existe' (*N*, p. 129). He simply exists as body; as mind, he exists because he thinks he exists. His thoughts are therefore just as much him as his body: 'Ma pensée, c'est *moi*'. In a sense, then, the body depends on the mind for its continued existence, since, if we could cease to think we should cease to exist.

But this is not, of course, possible. Consequently, we find ourselves in the position of being, as consciousness, responsible for the existence of our physical selves, while at the same time depending on our continued physical existence in order that we may continue to exist as consciousness. Hence the importance of the story of Lucienne, a little girl who has been raped and murdered, who thus exists and does not exist at the same time: 'Son corps existe encore, sa chair meurtrie. *Elle* n'existe plus' (*N*, p. 130). Although the maniac attacked her body, it is her mind that has ceased to exist.

This fact leads Roquentin to the conclusion that existence is an imperfection: on the one hand, the desire of which the rapist is *conscious* can be expressed only through the flesh (the *material* self); on the other hand, in a perfect being, it would be impossible to destroy the consciousness by an assault on the physical self. It leads also to confirmation of his view of those people he calls *salauds*: 'Le monsieur sent qu'il existe. Non, le beau monsieur qui passe, fier et doux comme un volubilis, ne sent pas qu'il existe. (. . .) Le beau monsieur existe Légion d'honneur, existe moustache, c'est tout' (*N*, p. 131). The gentleman reduces himself to a Legion of Honour and a moustache (and, of course, all that they represent) in order that he may have a clear definition of himself and to escape the implications of the unsatisfactory manner in which we in fact exist; the definable part of our existence is our body (ourself as object), whilst consciousness (what I consider to be the essential me) is something which cannot be defined. The *beau monsieur* takes refuge behind his decoration and his moustache; some defend themselves by constant reference to their experience; others justify themselves by a series of duties and rights: 'Il a la Légion d'honneur, les Salauds ont le droit d'exister: "j'existe parce que c'est mon droit" ' (*N*, p. 131). As for Roquentin, his inability to reconcile the two apparently incompatible modes of our existence lead him into a state of panic which ceases only when he goes into the 'Bar de la Marine'. Once again, he is delivered from his nausea by a piece of music. Earlier, listening to *Some of these days*, in the 'Rendez-vous des Cheminots', he had been struck by the way in which the music seemed to exist in a more necessary way than did the people in the café. Now, hearing *When the low moon begins to beam*, he has a similar impression, but is able to integrate it into the context of more recent events. He realises that the woman singing the song existed in the same way as he, or anyone else. 'Mais il y a ça. On ne peut pas dire que cela existe' (*N*, p. 132). Not, at any rate, in the usual way. *Ça* is, of course, the music, which somehow goes beyond the normal world of existence which includes people, objects—or even records: 'Moi, qui écoute, j'existe. Tout est plein, l'existence partout, dense et lourde et douce. Mais, par delà toute cette douceur, inaccessible, toute proche, si loin hélas, jeune, impitoyable et sereine il y a cette . . . cette rigueur' (*N*, p. 133). The music *does* exist, in other words, but in some special, more rigorous fashion, which Roquentin does not, for the moment, explain.

Instead, after a brief entry ('Rien. Existé'), which is a reflection of his continued inability to understand the *sense* of his existence, he is given the opportunity of approaching the problem from another direction during his lunch with the Autodidacte. Like the scene in the portrait-gallery, this is a brilliant set-piece description and, as such, provides its own rewards to the reader. It also contributes its share, however, to the development of the theme of the novel by revealing to us the reasons why the Autodidacte lives as he does. He is, in practice, every bit as solitary as Roquentin himself but will not accept the fact: his professed 'humanism' expresses his belief that we can find our justification in communion with other men and through the upholding of human 'values'. His ambition systematically to read all the books in the public library is the method by which he hopes to give meaning to his existence: for the moment he is in the process of cultivating himself; eventually he will *be* cultivated and will then participate in the whole of human achievement. Without realising it, the Autodidacte is the victim of the *salauds*: the values he so much respects are the ones by which they conceal from themselves the reality of their existence, and at the same time are what give them a large measure of influence over respectful beings such as the Autodidacte. His humanism is an echo of these values as well as his defence against solitude: it is another method, like a belief in rights or Experience, of labelling oneself along with others, and of giving oneself a place in the scheme of things. What the Autodidacte will not realise is that he is nonetheless completely superfluous; Roquentin sees it clearly, as a fact that applies no less to himself than to the Autodidacte: 'J'ai envie de partir, de m'en aller quelque part où je serais vraiment *à ma place*, où je m'emboîterais . . . Mais ma place n'est nulle part; je suis de trop' (*N*, p. 155). The obvious evidence of this fact, in contrast with the Auto-didacte's persistent humanism, revolts Roquentin to such an extent that it brings on another violent attack of nausea.

Things are beginning to fall into place. Roquentin now sees that the Autodidacte has revealed to him something of importance. During the course of keeping his diary, Roquentin has progressed from the undefined sensation he experienced on picking up the pebble, through an awareness that objects exist in a different way to himself, and on, finally, to a consciousness of the gap between our two conflicting modes of existence. Now he sees that nausea is no more than the realisation, in a fully conscious way, of the fact of existence: 'C'est donc ça la Nausée: cette aveuglante évidence? Me suis-je creusé la tête! En ai-je écrit! Maintenant je sais: J'existe—le monde existe—et je sais que le monde existe. C'est tout' (N, p. 156). This realisation does not, however, free him from nausea. The Autodidacte has the feeling of being in tune with the world because he applies to it the categories and values invented by men as a defence against that world. But what if, as is the case for Roquentin, those categories and values are no longer to be accepted? Can we even make any satisfactory use of words, which are the vehicles by which we transmit values, but which are also the labels that we, as men, attempt to attach to the objects of the material world? Once these questions are asked, nausea is reinforced because objects appear even more alien than before. If they free themselves from their names, they cease being individual objects and become no more than part of existence in general. Roquentin comes near to understanding this when, looking at the sea, he perceives it as something different, and possibly more menacing, than the reassuring green surface beyond which we do not normally penetrate. But the truth really begins to dawn when he gets into the tram, and finds that the seat will not, as it were, answer to its name: 'Je murmure: c'est une banquette, un peu comme un exorcisme. Mais le mot reste sur mes lèvres: il refuse d'aller se poser sur la chose. Elle reste ce qu'elle est' (N, p. 159). As Proust says in A l'ombre des jeunes filles en fleurs: 'Les noms qui désignent les choses répondent toujours à une notion de l'intelligence, étrangère à nos impressions véritables, et qui nous force à éliminer d'elles tout ce qui ne se rapporte pas à cette notion'.[1] Roquentin's present experience is that the part of things we eliminate when we name them is precisely the part which matters, for the simple reason that words do not exist in the same realm as objects and so cannot apply to what is specifically 'object' about them. 'Les choses', writes Roquentin, 'se sont délivrées de leurs noms. Elles sont là, grotesques,

---

[1] A la recherche du temps perdu (Pléiade edition), vol. I (Paris, 1954), p. 835.

têtues, géantes et ça paraît imbécile de les appeler des banquettes ou de
dire quoi que ce soit sur elles: je suis au milieu des Choses, les in-
nommables' (N, p. 159). And what goes for things can also go for people:
the automatism of the movements of the man opposite Roquentin de-
humanises him and makes him appear in the same light as a thing.
Roquentin can stand it no longer, and jumps off the tram.

But, at last, thanks to the divorce that has come about between words
and things, he thinks he has fully understood the meaning of all that has
happened since he first picked up the pebble on the beach. As he sits in
the park looking at the root of the chestnut tree, he is aware of it only as
a form of existence: 'Les mots s'étaient evanouis et, avec eux, la signi-
fication des choses, leurs modes d'emploi, les faibles repères que les
hommes ont tracés à leur surface' (N, p. 161). Normally, words act as a
screen between us and existence and therefore free us from the need to
know what we mean when we use the word 'exist'. Although we are
surrounded by existence, and are indeed part of it ourselves, our approach
to the world is made through descriptions, classifications, relationships,
etc., which, since they are expressed in *words*, can never in fact be attached
to *objects*. What Roquentin now sees is that, if we stop considering the
world as a series of named objects which surround us and which are at
our service, we are faced with nothing less than massive Existence:
'la diversité des choses, leur individualité n'était qu'une apparence, un
vernis. Ce vernis avait fondu, il restait des masses monstrueuses et
molles, en désordre—nues, d'une effrayante et obscène nudité' (N, p.
162). It is true, as earlier episodes would lead us to expect, that there is
another realm: 'Dans un autre monde, les cercles, les airs de musique
gardent leurs lignes pures et rigides' (N, p. 162). Anything which falls
short of the purity of the circle or the piece of music must exist in an
imperfect way. More than that, it does not even exist with any kind of
necessity. A chestnut tree can have a meaning for us only if we can
isolate it and give it a label; once it loses its individual status and becomes
absorbed into existence in general, it is superfluous, a fact that is as true
for a man as for a tree: 'De trop, le marronnier, là en face de moi un peu
sur la gauche. (. . .) Et *moi*—veule, alangui, obscène, digérant, ballottant
de mornes pensées—*moi aussi j'étais de trop*' (N, p. 163).

The climax of Roquentin's metaphysical experience has been reached.
Having recounted the scene in the park, he is led to an awareness of what
he calls the Absurd, and attempts to express why this word should be the
appropriate one to use:

Un cercle n'est pas absurde, il s'explique très bien par la rotation d'un segment de droite autour d'une de ses extrémités. Mais aussi un cercle n'existe pas. Cette racine, au contraire, existait dans la mesure où je ne pouvais pas l'expliquer. (. . .) Cette racine, avec sa couleur, sa forme, son mouvement figé, était . . . au-dessous de toute explication.

(N, p. 164)

This contrast fits into the context of what we have already seen. A circle is not absurd and can be explained because it is an abstract invention of the intelligence; abstract ideas can be reduced to rational formulation and so be understood by the intelligence. The tree-root, for its part, is beneath explanation for two reasons: explanations exist in the sphere of intelligence and that is not the sphere in which the tree-root exists; secondly, the tree-root, as part of Existence, is simply given and is therefore unexplainable. It is also, as we have seen, *de trop*, superfluous; its existence, in other words, is in no way necessary: 'L'essentiel c'est la contingence. Je veux dire que, par définition, l'existence n'est pas la nécessité. Exister, c'est *être là*, simplement; les existants apparaissent, se laissent *rencontrer*, mais on ne peut jamais les *déduire*' (N, p. 166). Perhaps if Roquentin were to discover something which *can* be deduced from something else, he would have found something which escapes the contingency of existence. For the moment, he fails to make such a discovery; although he attempts to do so by casting movement in this role, he quickly realises that movement itself cannot be isolated from the world of existence, in which, if anything happens to an object, the cause must be sought outside the object itself. This is true of the trees: 'Las et vieux, ils continuaient d'exister, de mauvaise grâce, simplement parce qu'ils étaient trop faibles pour mourir, parce que la mort ne pouvait leur venir que de l'extérieur'. But Roquentin adds: 'il n'y a que les airs de musique pour porter fièrement leur propre mort en soi comme une nécessité interne; seulement ils n'existent pas' (N, p. 169).

Having reached this point, Roquentin believes that he has learnt all that he can know about existence. In fact, however, the process he has been going through is not yet complete. For one thing, he has not succeeded in explaining the 'sorte d'air complice' of which he is aware as he leaves the park. In addition, it is clear that he cannot dispose of music by saying that it does not exist: the fact that it has already been linked with the notion of the circle, and that, on more than one occasion, relief from the experience of nausea has come as a result of listening to music, suggests that all has not yet been said on the subject. And in

any case, as we are about to see, his visit to Anny adds a further dimen-
sion to what he has already discovered, since it emerges that, during
the period of their separation, Anny, within the context of her own preoccupations, has been evolving in much the same way as Roquentin
himself. The parallel is brought out in Anny's explanation of what she
means by those *moments parfaits* by which she used to set such store but
in which she no longer believes. Her explanation shows, incidentally,
how close she comes to Sartre the boy in this respect. In our Introduction,
we quoted the passage in *Les Mots* in which Sartre claims that, for him,
the pictures in the *Grand Larousse* appeared truer than the things they
represented (the monkeys in the engravings were more monkeys than
the ones in the zoo, etc.). Anny had the same reaction before the illustrations in Michelet's *Histoire de France*: they shared, for example, a quality
common to the pictures in the encyclopædia or, indeed, the words in a
book—they could be counted on to appear at the place fixed for them.
But they possessed another characteristic that made Anny see them as the
representation of what she calls *situations privilégiées*: 'C'étaient des
situations qui avaient une qualité tout à fait rare et précieuse, du style, si
tu veux' (*N*, p. 185). The events illustrated did not seem to her to be
necessarily of the greatest historical importance, or even those that lent
themselves most obviously to pictorial representation. She therefore
concluded that they must have some special nature which transformed
them into situations privileged to be used as illustrations.

One thing they very often represented was death, and this led Anny
to believe that death must be one of the things tending to produce a
privileged situation. Consequently, at the death of her father, she thinks
that her opportunity may have come actually to *live* a *situation privilégiée*
for herself. She is disappointed: she sees her mother and her aunt weeping
at the bedside, but nothing more; although she tries to view the situation
as a privileged one, she finds it impossible to do so, and comes to the
conclusion that it is essential to make a *situation privilégiée* give rise to a
moment parfait: 'Il y a d'abord des signes annonciateurs. Puis la situation
privilégiée, lentement, majestueusement, entre dans la vie des gens. Alors
la question se pose de savoir si on veut en faire un moment parfait' (*N*,
p. 186). She agrees with Roquentin that the situation provides the
material which must be worked if it is to produce a perfect moment;
but she will not accept his suggestion that a perfect moment is a work of
art. For her it is more a duty: 'Il *fallait* transformer les situations privilégiées en moments parfaits. C'était une question de morale' (*N*, p. 187).

What is clear, at any rate, is the analogy between perfect moments and adventures, if only in the negative sense that neither can exist in real life. Just as adventures can exist only as stories, that is to say in retrospect, so a perfect moment can only be identified as such if it is not part of a situation in the process of being lived. Anny thought that, by acting in a certain way, by going through that ritual which Roquentin could never understand, the perfect moment of love, or hate, or death would be realised: 'Je croyais qu'on pouvait rayonner de haine ou de mort. Quelle erreur! (. . .) Naturellement il n'y a que moi, moi qui hais, moi qui aime. Et alors ça, moi, c'est toujours la même chose, une pâte qui s'allonge, qui s'allonge . . .' (N, p. 189).

Both Anny and Roquentin have thus arrived at the realisation that the existence of the physical world and of themselves as part of that world is a fact which must inhibit any aspiration they may have to create something absolute. As Anny points out, however, they have been led to this realisation by following different paths:

> Tu sais, quand nous jouions à l'aventurier et à l'aventurière: toi tu étais celui à qui il arrive des aventures, moi j'étais celle qui les fait arriver. Je disais: "Je suis un homme d'action." Tu te rappelles? Eh bien, je dis simplement à présent: on ne peut pas être un homme d'action.
>
> (N, p. 190)

Roquentin expected adventures to happen to him; Anny wanted to make adventures (and later perfect moments) come about. Anny has arrived at the end of her evolution; her desire to produce events which should go beyond the limits of ordinary existence has proved to be an ambition that cannot be realised. If action cannot produce the hoped for results, then a life of action has no more point: ' "Je me . . . je me survis", répète-t-elle lourdement' (N, p. 190). She will simply allow herself to be kept by the man who is living with her, and will attempt to 'arrange' her past life, to organise it into some sort of pattern.

Roquentin, for his part, is in no such *impasse*. When he suggested that the perfect moment was a work of art, Anny was right to disagree, no doubt. Roquentin was, nevertheless, thinking along the right lines in the sense that perfect moments, adventures, and works of art all exist outside the contingent world in which we live. It will be remembered that, before leaving Bouville, Roquentin had seen the *non-existence* of music as a reason for not being able to consider it as a useful example of

something which escapes contingency. Now, returning to a consider-
ation of the work of art in general, he is perhaps given a clue to the defect in his own reasoning when Anny speaks about her attempts to realise
perfect moments in the theatre, which Sartre himself will frequently
speak of in terms of ritual. If a perfect moment existed for anyone,
she says, it could only be for the members of the audience:

> Mais, tu sais, ils ne vivaient pas dedans: il se déroulait devant eux. Et
> nous, les acteurs, tu penses que nous vivions dedans? Finalement il
> n'était nulle part, ni d'un côté ni de l'autre de la rampe, il n'existait
> pas; et pourtant tout le monde pensait à lui.
>
> (N, p. 191)

Perhaps, in other words, the work of art exists in a manner different
from that we normally know in the contingent world. Is it possible, for
example, for every one in a theatre to think about something (the
perfect moment referred to above) if it does not exist in one way or
another?

Whatever the answer, it is not immediately provided. Roquentin and
Anny have said all they had to say to each other; each is no more than
part of the other's past. Now that he has 'lost' both Anny and M. de
Rollebon and that he is on the point of leaving Bouville, Roquentin
has the feeling that he is both alone and completely disengaged from the
world: 'Aujourd'hui ma vie prend fin', he writes, 'Toute ma vie est
derrière moi' (N, pp. 196, 197). He thinks that, from now on, like Anny,
he will merely survive, but before the remaining ties are cut by his final
departure from Bouville, he will do two last things: take one more
walk to look at the town, and return the books he has borrowed from the
library. Looking down on Bouville, he is brought back to his reflections
on the town and the people in it. They, like their predecessors perpetuated on the walls of the portrait-gallery, are confident that the
world is as they see it and remain unaware of Existence such as it has
imposed itself upon Roquentin's consciousness. What would they do if
things no longer appeared in their usual guise, if objects suddenly under-
went monstrous transformations, or if, more simply, people suddenly
became aware of 'une espèce de sens affreux, lourdement posé sur les
choses' (N, p. 200)? When that day comes and men are brought, like
Roquentin, face to face with the reality of Existence, he knows what his
reaction will be: 'Je m'adosserai à un mur et je leur crierai au passage:
"Qu'avez-vous fait de votre science? Qu'avez-vous fait de votre human-

isme? Où est votre dignité de roseau pensant?" ' (*N*, p. 200). Where, indeed? The answer is given, in a sense, by the Autodidacte, whose faith in knowledge, humanism, man's dignity as a 'thinking reed' has hitherto been complete. Caught in the act of making advances to a schoolboy in the public library, he is humiliated, struck, and expelled from the library: he has, in other words, been rejected by those men in whom he put his faith, and separated from the Science which guaranteed their values and also, he hoped, justified himself. Mankind is not so much a thinking reed as a broken one: it has failed to give him the support he needed, and left him more alone than he already was: 'Je regrette de ne pas l'avoir accompagné', writes Roquentin, 'mais il ne l'a pas voulu; c'est lui qui m'a supplié de le laisser seul: il commençait l'apprentissage de la solitude' (*N*, p. 201).

Roquentin is no less a solitary figure, but at least he has not been deprived of all that seemed to give meaning to his life. He can even enjoy his present situation, in which he is as detached as is possible from his surroundings: 'Je savoure cet oubli total où je suis tombé. Je suis entre deux villes, l'une m'ignore, l'autre ne me connaît plus' (*N*, p. 211). Indeed, he begins to realise that he is so completely forgotten that he can no longer be sure of his own identity: 'A présent, quand de dis "je", ça me semble creux' (*N*, p. 212). The more the full impact of his detachment bears in on him, the more he loses his sense of self, until finally, 'le Je pâlit, pâlit et c'en est fait, il s'éteint' (*N*, p. 212). And yet consciousness remains, if only as *consciousness that* the *Je* has faded away, if only as consciousness that consciousness itself is *de trop*. Consciousness therefore knows itself as unattached, but always conscious *of* something: the street, a shop, Anny, a song. It recovers its 'identity' as, finding himself before the 'Rendez-vous des Cheminots', Roquentin springs back into consciousness, and the two coincide once again. This renewed coincidence does not prevent either Roquentin or his consciousness from being *de trop*. It looks as though he must, whether he likes it or not, be reduced to the same state as Anny: that of simply surviving. After all, there is nothing to be gained by activity in the world: 'faire quelque chose, c'est créer de l'existence—et il y a bien assez d'existence comme ça' (*N*, p. 216).

Thus Roquentin has reached a low state, and accepts without enthusiasm when the café waitress offers to play the record of *Some of these days*. Music can provide no consolation, he thinks; indeed, he despises those who romantically believe that beauty can compensate for their humiliations or their suffering. Music, or any other form of art, does not exist in the real world and therefore cannot act upon the real world. We have already noted that, for Roquentin, music does not exist. He still thinks this to be true, and yet he is puzzled and irritated. He hears the melody, but it does not exist; if he were to break the record, a thing which *does* exist, he would therefore have no effect on the melody, because it is always somehow *beyond* the world accessible to us: 'quand on veut la saisir, on ne rencontre que des existants, on bute sur des existants dépourvus de sens.' Perhaps, however, as we saw when speaking of *L'Imaginaire*, it is a mistake to apply to the melody the usual criteria of existence. Roquentin begins to have some inkling of this possibility when he writes: 'Elle n'existe pas, puisqu'elle n'a rien de trop: c'est tout le reste qui est trop par rapport à elle. Elle *est*.' And he adds: 'Et moi aussi j'ai voulu *être*' (*N*, p. 218). He *exists* in the world of gramophone records; he would like to *be* in the world of music: 'de l'autre côté de l'existence, dans cet autre monde qu'on peut voir de loin, mais sans jamais l'approcher'; in the world of characters in paintings or in novels; in the realm of beings who have been created, who *are*, but who do not exist in this contingent world; in the world of the imaginary.

It is the realm of *Some of these days*. The scratch on the record is a defect in the record, but has no effect whatever on the song. The record will be damaged, will become broken, will disappear: 'Mais derrière l'existant qui tombe d'un présent à l'autre, sans passé, sans avenir, derrière ces sons qui, de jour en jour, se décomposent, s'écaillent et glissent vers la mort, la mélodie reste la même, jeune et ferme, comme un témoin sans pitié' (*N*, p. 219). And yet this song, which exists beyond the contingent world, was created by a man no less *de trop* than Roquentin himself: a fat American, who was short of money, had other human problems, and who, nevertheless, created this melody which, since it exists in its inevitable, necessary way, bestows upon its creator some of its own necessity and helps him, at any rate partially, to escape from his contingency. And what is true of the Jewish composer is also true of the negress who sings the song:

> En voilà deux qui sont sauvés: le Juif et la Négresse. Sauvés. Ils se sont peut-être cru perdus jusqu'au bout, noyés dans l'existence. Et pourtant, personne ne pourrait penser à moi comme je pense à eux, avec cette douceur. Personne, pas même Anny. Ils sont un peu pour moi comme des morts, un peu comme des héros de roman; ils se sont lavés du péché d'exister.
>
> (*N*, p. 221)

Cleansed of the sin of existing because, as we have seen, existence is an imperfection, whereas music is pure and free from the imperfection of existence in a contingent world. By composing the song and singing it, the Jew and the negress have created something which exists in a pure and necessary way that can only be possible beyond the contingent world; and by producing the song whose existence is necessary, the composer and the singer must also, to some extent, have a necessary existence.

'Alors on peut justifier son existence?' (*N*, p. 221), Roquentin asks himself. Perhaps it will be possible for him to exist necessarily, and so to escape from the contingency which gave rise to nausea. He will not achieve the aim by writing music, since he is not a composer. Writing is the means at his disposal, but not the writing of history: he now realises that he made a mistake in trying to resuscitate M. de Rollebon and to see him as a justification: 'jamais un existant ne peut justifier l'existence d'un autre existant' (*N*, p. 222). This is obvious enough: a contingent being cannot free another contingent being from its contingency. Hence Roquentin's conclusion that he should perhaps write a novel: 'il faudrait qu'on devine, derrière les mots imprimés, derrière les pages, quelque chose qui n'existerait pas, qui serait au-dessus de l'existence. Une histoire, par exemple, comme il ne peut pas en arriver, une aventure.' A biography of M. de Rollebon would have been a book about another contingent being; by writing *Le Rouge et le Noir*, Stendhal created, in Julien Sorel, a character who, although he may give the illusion of having existed as a contingent human being, could never in fact exist in such a way: Julien, in this respect, resembles the circle, the piece of music, the triangle. If Roquentin were to write a novel, he would be in the same situation as Stendhal, or the creators of *Some of these days*:

> Et il y aurait des gens qui liraient ce roman et qui diraient: "C'est Antoine Roquentin qui l'a écrit, c'était un type roux qui traînait dans les cafés", et ils penseraient à ma vie comme je pense à celle de cette négresse: comme à quelque chose de précieux et d'à moitié légendaire.
>
> (*N*, p. 222)

He, too, by the creation of a work of art owing its existence to his imagination, would be cleansed of the sin of existing.

Les Mouches

Ce n'est pas dans je ne sais quelle retraite que
nous nous découvrirons: c'est sur la route,
dans la ville, au milieu de la foule, chose
parmi les choses, homme parmi les hommes.[1]

An analysis of *La Nausée* makes clear the similarities between Roquentin and the Sartre described in *Les Mots*. Both seek to justify themselves through writing; both think it possible, through the creation of works of the imagination, to bestow upon themselves a necessity they do not otherwise have; both attempt to cleanse themselves of the 'sin of existence' in the world of other men. One can therefore see how there is some truth in Sartre's assertion of 1964: 'En face d'un enfant qui meurt, *la Nausée* ne fait pas le poids.' Roquentin's reaction to the revelation of his own superfluousness is to look for a salvation which will at the same time owe nothing to anyone but himself and exist outside the world in which we actually have to live. The solution is metaphysical, but also solipsistic, and thus well suited to the pre-war Sartre, whose awareness of the world about him did not seem to impose the need to become involved in the important issues which confronted him as a member of society. The war brought about a rapid change in Sartre's own attitude; writing about a week they spent together in February 1940, Simone de Beauvoir says this of him: 'il était bien décidé à ne plus se tenir à l'écart de la vie politique. Sa nouvelle morale, basée sur la notion d'authenticité, et qu'il s'efforçait de mettre en pratique, exigeait que l'homme "assumât" sa "situation".'[2] The extent to which, in practice, he could assume his situation was no doubt limited by the fact that he was taken prisoner by the Germans only four months after the leave to which Simone de Beauvoir refers. A result of his imprisonment, however, was the revelation to him of the theatre as a place in which men are involved with other men. It would not be appropriate to this study to examine Sartre's

[1] 'Une idée fondamentale de Husserl', *op. cit.*, pp. 34–5.
[2] *La Force de l'âge* (Paris, 1960), p. 442.

approach to the theatre in general;[1] all we need do is to note the fact that he wrote and put on his first play before his fellow-prisoners at the end of 1940. He has described his own reaction to this experience in the following terms: 'as I addressed my comrades across the foot-lights, speaking to them of their state as prisoners, when I suddenly saw them so remarkably silent and attentive, I realised what the theatre ought to be —a great collective religious phenomenon.'[2] The word *collective* is of great importance. The novel, as we saw in the case of Roquentin, is a largely solitary form: it is written by one man and read by an individual. The same thing cannot be said of a play. Although, like the novel, it is an imaginary work of art written (normally) by one man, it differs from the novel in the vital respect that it cannot be concerned only with establishing a link between the author and the realm of the ideal. For Sartre, the author of a play can never lose sight of other men, the collection of people before whom the play will actually be acted.

Seen in this light, writing for the theatre is an activity towards which one might in any case have expected Sartre to move. If *Les Mots* reveals to us a small boy who turned to writing in order to justify his own existence, it does not follow that it shows us merely a junior version of Roquentin; both may indeed be *de trop*, but Sartre presents his own childhood problem as being a human, rather than a metaphysical, one: he was *de trop* in relation to the people around him, and more especially to his grandfather. He writes partly in order to impose himself upon the attention of others, and the theatre is a potentially more satisfactory medium than the novel for this purpose. Not only that, but a play, by its nature, is a representation of men acting together within a given context (at least in the theatrical convention exploited by Sartre), and this means that their preoccupations cannot involve the kind of radical isolation from other people that we find in *La Nausée*. If, therefore, we may expect Sartre to continue the examination of themes which already existed in his pre-war work, his subsequent involvement in the affairs of the world, combined with his move towards work in the theatre, would suggest that those themes will henceforth be worked out within a social framework of one kind or another. *Les Mouches* is a good example of the way in which this evolution takes place, but it should be added

[1] On this subject, see my article: 'The Theatre of Sartre: 1940–1965', *Books Abroad*, vol. 41, no 2 (Spring 1967), pp. 133–49.
[2] 'Forgers of Myths: the young playwrights of France', *Theatre Arts* (June 1946), p. 330.

that we are not therefore obliged to see this play, any more than those which follow it (with the *possible* exception of *La Putain respectueuse*), as direct comment on precise events in the contemporary world: Sartre's notion of committed literature does not include the idea that an author should recommend taking up a given attitude to a given problem. For that reason alone it would be inappropriate to see *Les Mouches*, produced in 1943, as a play aiming to encourage resistance to the German occupation of France: to find a precise political *message* in the play is to transform it into a *pièce à thèse*, and it has never been Sartre's ambition to produce that kind of literature. In fact, if one wishes to discover in the play a character who may be taken to represent Resistance, that character can only be Electre;[1] but the difficulty about her is that, once she is free of the tyrants, she falls into the very attitudes that she previously condemned in them. As for Oreste, he can in no way be taken to symbolise the Resistance: he is the 'liberator' who comes from outside and who is not himself involved in the situation of Argos; and if we put the word *liberator* in inverted commas, it is precisely because, as we shall see, his 'liberation' of the people of Argos is ambiguous in nature and bound up with the inauthentic character of his final attitude.

Nevertheless, the fact that it is possible for us to write in terms of involvement indicates the extent to which the main character of *Les Mouches* differs from Roquentin and reflects a side of Sartre not represented by Roquentin. Both characters are isolated from people around them and both have a feeling of being *de trop*, superfluous in terms of the world in which they live. Roquentin's experience is no doubt partly the result of his lack of relationships with others, but the form it takes, as we have seen, is metaphysical, and the solution he foresees is of a kind which need, as *L'Imaginaire* suggests, owe nothing to other men. Oreste is closer to Sartre himself in that he is aware of himself as being *de trop* with regard to other people and the group which they go to make up. Just as Sartre turned to writing as a means of asserting his own autonomous existence in the face of his family, so Oreste will seek a means by which he may make a place for himself in the community of men. *Les Mouches* is the story of his struggle to achieve his aim; our task will be to see how he carries on that struggle and to decide how far he is successful in his ambition.

It would be wrong to assume that Oreste arrives in Argos with any

[1]We shall, as a matter of convenience, retain the French form of the characters' names.

specific intentions about possible action in the city. The evidence of the play is that, having learnt of his true identity as the son of the assassinated king of Argos, Agamemnon, he returns to his native town more to see the place in which he was born than to avenge his father's death or to claim the throne of Argos as his own: there is no reason to think that he is anything less than sincere when, in answer to Jupiter's talk about the unstable equilibrium of the town, he replies: 'cela ne me regarde pas' (*M*, p. 21).[1] This is, indeed, what one might expect: we are told that the soldiers ordered to kill him after the assassination of Agamemnon took pity on him and abandoned him in the forest; he was discovered there and brought up 'par de riches bourgeois d'Athènes' (*M*, p. 19). We are given no more information about these adoptive parents, and are clearly intended to take it that they neither had a formative influence on him nor provided him with a human context he could recognise as his own. His sole mentor appears to have been the Pédagogue, and, at the beginning of the play, Oreste speaks as though he has absorbed a fair amount of his ideal of detachment from the everyday world, even if he has arrived at the stage of being dissatisfied with it.

The point emerges with some clarity in their scene together after Jupiter's departure: their confrontation shows the contrast between what the Pédagogue has tried to make of Oreste, and what Oreste has the impression of being—or more precisely of *not* being. The Pédagogue's teaching has been a form of eclecticism, combining the 'scepticisme souriant' (*M*, p. 22) of a Renan and the detachment of the intellectual with elements drawn from the attitudes of the Autodidacte and the *salauds* of La Nausée. He claims that his education has provided Oreste with all that a young man should wish for: wide knowledge in the fields of history, geography, archaeology, etc.; extensive reading ('Ne vous ai-je pas fait, de bonne heure, lire tous les livres . . .'); a whole culture, lovingly composed, says the Pédagogue, of the fruits of his wisdom and the treasures of his experience. All this with a view to producing Oreste as he now is: 'A présent vous voilà jeune, riche et beau, avisé comme un vieillard, affranchi de toutes les servitudes et de toutes les croyances, sans famille, sans patrie, sans religion, sans métier, libre pour tous les engagements et sachant qu'il ne faut jamais s'engager' (*M*, pp. 23–4). The Pédagogue, like Dr Rogé in La Nausée, would like to think that he can distill his own past Experience into a Wisdom that he can pass on to Oreste. But Oreste cannot agree: one man's memories can never make

---

[1] Jean-Paul Sartre, *Les Mouches*, in *Théâtre* (Paris, Gallimard, 1947).

another man's past, as Roquentin had already pointed out: 'Le passé,
c'est un luxe de propriétaire. (. . .) Je ne possède que mon corps; un
homme tout seul, avec son seul corps, ne peut pas arrêter les souvenirs;
ils lui passent au travers. Je ne devrais pas me plaindre: je n'ai voulu
qu'être libre' (N, p. 88). Roquentin, of course, not only *had* wanted to
remain free, but also, at the end of his diary, envisaged a future which
would enable him to remain free.

It is not the kind of freedom which attracts Oreste: beliefs, family,
country, religion, occupation—all those things of which he has remained
independent are precisely the ones that could give a meaning to his
existence: 'Moi, je suis libre, Dieu merci', he says ironically. 'Ah!
comme je suis libre. Et quelle superbe absence que mon âme' (M, p. 24).
His freedom makes him like a wisp of gossamer floating in the air—
insubstantial and unattached; his freedom is not so much a liberation as
an exile. Some men are born committed (*engagés*) and therefore have
their path traced out for them. The world has a meaning for them and
their past has some significance because the two are not divorced. Oreste
is differently placed: since he does not act in the world, the events of
that world do not concern him and cannot provide those memories
which give us a sense of identity and continuity: 'Car les souvenirs sont
de grasses nourritures pour ceux qui possèdent les maisons, les bêtes,
les domestiques et les champs' (M, p. 24). The different ways in which the
same idea is used by Oreste and Roquentin ('Le passé, c'est un luxe de
propriétaire') is a good indication of the contrast between them. Roquentin associates property, memories, and the past with those people he
calls *salauds* because such people use their past as a justification for their
present and as a defence against the fact of their own lack of necessity.
Oreste, on the other hand, sees memories as an element in a past which is
shared with other people and which gives the individual a place *amongst
men*. When he looks at the royal palace in Argos, he sees only an example
of a given architectural and decorative style, and not a building having
the kind of meaning which can only come from its human function—
as the place, for example, in which he, as son of Agamemnon, might
have grown up. For the people of Argos, of course, the palace is more
than a piece of architecture because it is one of the points around which
their life in common has centred, and in which they see a reflection of
their past life—happy or unhappy, good or bad:

Mais quoi? qu'ai-je à faire avec ces gens? Je n'ai pas vu naître un seul
de leurs enfants, ni assisté aux noces de leurs filles, je ne partage pas

leurs remords et je ne connais pas un seul de leurs noms. C'est le barbu [Jupiter] qui a raison : un roi doit avoir les mêmes souvenirs que ses sujets.

(*M*, p. 26)

Oreste sees that he has no place in Argos, and yet he *is* the son of Agamemnon, thinks that he should have a place in the city, and wonders whether, despite everything, it might not be possible to make a place for himself in Argos by becoming involved with its past. The terms he uses are significant for the future development of the action: 'si je pouvais m'emparer, fût-ce par un crime, de leurs mémoires, de leur terreur et de leurs espérances pour combler le vide de mon cœur, dussé-je tuer ma propre mère . . .' (*M*, p. 26). He is indeed free, but now feels the need to be free *for* something—such as an act which will make him a part of Argos. And it should be noted that, at the end of this important scene, although Oreste considers that his freedom should be used, he is concerned to employ it in his own interest and in no way as a means of serving the people of Argos.

The scene which we have just examined reveals an Oreste conscious of a need to 'belong', but not committed to any action designed to satisfy that need. The rest of the first Act, along with the first Tableau in Act II, will show how the effect upon him of encounters with his sister and his mother, followed by the 'Fête des morts', lead him to decide that he will remain in Argos and that he will carry through the assassination of Egisthe and Clytemnestre. Electre and Clytemnestre both, in their different ways, give Oreste reasons for staying in Argos, and both reveal something of the attitudes current in the city. The opening scene of the play, through the old woman, had already shown a people crushed under the weight of repentance and remorse for the killing of Agamemnon. Electre does not share their feelings; she is motivated by hatred of her father's assassins and by impatience to see her brother return, convinced as she is that he will come to avenge his father's death and to discredit Jupiter, less a god than a bogey-man whose function is to keep the people enslaved by fear and remorse. Addressing the statue of Jupiter, she says: 'il viendra, celui que j'attends, avec sa grande épée. Il te regardera en rigolant, comme ça, les mains sur les hanches et renversé en arrière. Et puis il tirera son sabre et il te fendra de haut en bas' (*M*, p. 28). Electre is at any rate one person in Argos who would welcome Oreste to the city (it should be remembered that her brother is still, for the moment, going under an assumed name), and who would

D

expect him to become involved in its affairs. Clytemnestre reveals that, for her too, Oreste continues to be of consequence: the one action for which she feels remorse is her failure to prevent Egisthe from handing her son over to the mercenaries who were ordered to kill him. His continued importance for Electre and Clytemnestre still does not cause in Oreste any resolve to action; but he does, at least, decide to stay in Argos to observe the 'Fête des morts'.

The ceremony is an extension of the scene which has just taken place. Clytemnestre's confession of remorse with respect to Oreste comes during a discussion which on the whole shows her in a very different light. She is like those *salauds* in *La Nausée* who hid from the fact that their existence was no more necessary or justified than that of a Roquentin by assuming a persona likely to give them an appearance of being indispensable: they played the role of The Doctor, The Grandfather, The Captain of Industry, or whatever was appropriate. Roquentin reproached them, not with playing a part which did not correspond to their function (Dr Rogé *was* a physician), but with behaving as though that function bestowed some absolute justification upon them. In *L'Etre et le néant*, published in the same year as *Les Mouches* was produced, Sartre defines this attitude as one of *mauvaise foi* ('bad faith'). From a philosophical point of view the concept of *mauvaise foi* involves the working out of some of the implications of the attitude already illustrated in *La Nausée*; in terms of characters created by Sartre, *Les Mouches* marks a corresponding step forward. Dr Rogé's *mauvaise foi* arises out of his desire to see his function as a doctor transformed into a kind of label which will characterise him once and for all; Clytemnestre is in a state of *mauvaise foi* because the label she wants to attach to herself does not necessarily correspond to any kind of truth. Sartre writes: 'La mauvaise foi a (. . .) en apparence la structure du mensonge. Seulement, ce qui change tout, c'est que, dans la mauvaise foi, c'est à moi-même que je masque la vérité.'[1] The truth is that Clytemnestre feels guilty of the supposed death of her son; but in order to hide this unpleasant fact from herself, in the first place, and consequently from those around her, she behaves in a way designed to force upon other people an image of herself as the woman who collaborated in the assassination of her husband and who now shares the bed of her husband's murderer. When she meets Oreste, therefore, she is only too glad to go through the process of self-accusation before him. After all, people are more likely to believe us when

[1] Jean-Paul Sartre, *L'Etre et le néant* (Paris, 1943), p. 87.

we confess our faults than when we proclaim our virtues, and Clytemnestre is concerned that no attempt should be made to go beyond the image she herself wishes to project:

> *Clytemnestre:* (. . .)   N'importe qui peut me cracher au visage, en m'appelant criminelle et prostituée. Mais personne n'a le droit de juger mes remords.
> *Electre:* Tu vois, Philèbe: c'est la règle du jeu. Les gens vont t'implorer pour que tu les condamnes. Mais prends bien garde de ne les juger que sur les fautes qu'ils t'avouent: les autres ne regardent personne, et ils te sauraient mauvais gré de les découvrir.

> (*M*, p. 36)

The people of Argos are in a different position, since they, in a sense, have their *mauvaise foi* thrust upon them. The old woman in the first scene of the play tells how her seven year-old grandson, born eight years after the death of Agamemnon, is nevertheless being brought up in the belief that he should feel remorse for the assassination. Now, as the crowd waits for the 'Fête des morts' to start, they show that they in fact fear the dead who, they believe, are about to be released, and they inculcate into their children the idea that this fear is something which should be felt by all right-thinking people: 'Il faut avoir peur, mon chéri. Grand'peur. C'est comme cela qu'on devient un honnête homme' (*M*, p. 41). But a belief in the virtues of fear and remorse depends on the authority of Egisthe, backed in theory by Jupiter. Certainly it could not be held that the arguments he brings to bear carry any great conviction; during the ceremonial, for example, he says this: 'Ne savez-vous pas que les morts n'ont jamais de pitié? Leurs griefs sont ineffaçables, parce que leur compte s'est arrêté pour toujours' (*M*, p. 47). If it is true that death has closed their account, then any pity or grievances which may have been important when the account was still open can no longer be of any consequence. Similarly in the case of the following remark: 'Les morts ne sont plus—comprenez-vous ce mot implacable—ils ne sont plus, et c'est pour cela qu'ils se sont faits les gardiens incorruptibles de vos crimes' (*M*, p. 48). It seems curious that Egisthe should insist on the fact that the dead no longer exist if he nevertheless wishes to convince people both that they exist as guardians of the crimes of the living and that they return to earth for one day each year. Perhaps this is why it is relatively easy for Electre, when she comes on the scene, to disrupt the ceremony and to start winning the people over to the belief that the dead are indeed dead and therefore cannot exert any effect on the living. It is significant that, faced with this situation, they do not turn to some transcendent power for guidance, but want to know how Egisthe defends his own authority: 'Menacer n'est pas répondre, Egisthe! N'as-tu rien d'autre à nous dire?' (*M*, p. 53). And it is doubtless no less significant that the miracle which saves him and makes it possible to ban Electre from Argos is one worked by Jupiter.

As far as Electre is concerned, the situation she has created by her defiance puts her in the position of not knowing what course of action to follow: if she stays in Argos, she will probably be put to death, but there are two reasons which make her refuse to flee. In the first place, to leave Argos would be to abandon the idea of avenging her father's death. Up to this time, her life has made sense only in terms of her hatred of Egisthe and Clytemnestre and of the desire to see them meet their death: vengeance, such as she envisages it, is a strictly personal matter, her own *raison d'être* rather than a means of bringing her father's assassins to justice: 'C'est tout ce que je demandais, Philèbe, je te le jure. (. . .) C'est que le sage ne peut rien souhaiter sur terre, sinon de rendre un jour le mal qu'on lui a fait' (*M*, p. 56). She reproaches Oreste with having made her forget her hatred, and therefore with having deprived her of what she calls her only treasure. Her second reason for being unwilling to flee is the one which will bring Oreste to the point of deciding what he will do. As a descendant of Atreus, she believes that her tragic destiny must be worked out in Argos, and forecasts that Oreste will be no more able than herself to avoid playing out his part. When he, however, reveals to her his true identity, her certainty is shaken, since she cannot believe that the gentle young man she knows is capable of carrying out an act of violence: 'j'aurais préféré que tu restes Philèbe et que mon frère fût mort' (*N*, p. 58). Now, it is Oreste who takes the initiative: we have already seen that both Electre and Clytemnestre had shown that he was not totally excluded from Argos, if only because he was present in their minds. Electre's conviction that her brother is destined by birth to be involved in the affairs of the city suggests that his place awaits him there. But the place, in Sartrean terms, has still to be made: for the moment, he does not have the consistency of a real man occupying a real place in a real community: 'de tous les fantômes qui rôdent aujourd'hui par la ville, aucun n'est plus fantôme que moi' (*M*, p. 60). He does not, for example, share Electre's hatred; as a result, Argos is no different from any other town in the sense that, if he left it, he would leave no trace of his passage and no sense of loss in its inhabitants. It is for this reason vital that he should remain in Argos, even at the risk of bringing about tragedy for others and possibly also for himself. 'Comprends-moi', he says to Electre, 'je veux être un homme de quelque part, un homme parmi les hommes' (*M*, p. 61). Even so, he is not finally committed to undertaking some action designed to give him his place amongst the people of Argos. Indeed, he goes so far as to call upon Zeus to guide him, on the grounds that his ambition has always been to serve the Good and that, in his present situation, he needs divine inspiration to know what the Good actually is.

Jupiter, unfortunately for himself, is over-anxious, and too ready to produce a sign supposed to persuade Oreste that the right course of action is one of humility and obedience to the laws of conventional behaviour. The sign is too clear; instead of convincing Oreste, it serves to make him aware of the sort of distance between himself and the everyday world that Roquentin had already observed. Instead of filling a gap, Jupiter's sign has opened one up: 'Il y avait autour de moi quelque chose de vivant et de chaud. Quelque chose qui vient de mourir. Comme tout est vide . . .' (*M*, p. 63). Like Roquentin, Oreste has understood that there is no coincidence between himself and the world about him; unlike Roquentin, he does not opt for a solitary solution but for a means whereby he can force himself into the world which surrounds him. His tendency is towards a solution of violence, which will allow him to impose his attentions upon the city, as the male is sometimes inclined to force his attentions upon the unwilling or the indifferent female: '(la ville) est à prendre, je le sens depuis ce matin. Et toi aussi, Electre, tu es à prendre. Je vous prendrai' (*M*, p. 64). The particular way in which he will impress himself upon the city is by assuming the crimes and the remorse of its inhabitants: in doing so, he will not only appear as the man who frees Argos from its guilt, but will also, by the action of assuming responsibility for the peoples' crimes, earn for himself a central place in their existence. Electre is convinced: Oreste is, after all, the Oreste she was waiting for; one might say that, in her eyes, what Anny would have called a *situation privilégiée* has been created:

j'ai peur—comme en songe. O moment tant attendu et tant redouté! A présent, les instants vont s'enchaîner comme les rouages d'une mécanique, et nous n'aurons plus de répit jusqu'à ce qu'ils soient couchés tous les deux sur le dos, avec des visages pareils à des mûres écrasées.

(*M*, p. 66)

Unfortunately, as in the case of Anny, this *situation privilégiée* will fail to give rise to a *moment parfait*—and for the same reasons.

The decision to kill Egisthe and Clytemnestre has been taken, but it still has to be carried into effect. The beginning of the second Tableau in Act II shows Egisthe himself in such a state of weariness that it is not certain that he would want to defend himself against actual physical attack. He is worn down by the knowledge that his hold over the people depends on a trick and that he will be lost if ever they succeed in seeing through that trick. He is condemned to play a part—to such an extent that he is almost persuaded by his own inventions, and is ready to believe that the dead Agamemnon has indeed come back to earth for the day. Jupiter, observing Egisthe's state, and knowing Oreste's intentions, sees the need to stiffen Egisthe's resolve. The scene in which he tries to achieve this is of interest from more than one point of view: it gives us the opportunity of seeing how Sartre the atheist presents a god to us; it shows the fundamental weakness of both divine and temporal power; and it makes clear the way in which man's freedom is more powerful than those forces which attempt to diminish its importance. As an atheist, Sartre does not, of course, believe in the existence of Jupiter any more than of any other god—just as, in writing *Huis-clos*, he did not believe in hell. Consequently, the references in both cases are strictly human. Like hell, Jupiter is a useful dramatic hypothesis which Sartre is able to exploit. Jupiter can indeed be no more than the bogey-man that Electre accuses him of being in the first Act; his existence resembles that of an imaginary object: neither is more real than the other. It is therefore difficult to accept some of the remarks he makes. 'Je t'ai dit que tu es fait à mon image', he says to Egisthe. 'Nous faisons tous les deux régner l'ordre, toi, dans Argos, moi dans le monde' (*M*, p. 77). Although the first sentence may not be open to particular objection, the second is conceivably inconsistent within its own terms, since Argos is presumably part of the world in which Jupiter claims to make order reign. But is such a claim in itself one which we should accept? It is true that he has a way with flies and knows how to produce interesting effects during public ceremonies, but he himself does not seem to look upon such accomplishments as more than parlour tricks; if he were able effectively to intervene in the world he would not need to call upon Egisthe to help him in frustrating the action contemplated by Oreste. In this context, the word *liberty* takes on a specifically Sartrean sense. Sartre insists not only that men are free, but also that they are condemned to be free, and we must understand this idea in the sense that any attempt to escape the consequences of that freedom will involve some kind of *mauvaise foi,* some attempt to live in a way which is inauthentic in human terms. Within this context, it becomes possible to understand the discussion of human liberty that takes place between Jupiter and Egisthe. Jupiter points out to Egisthe that they share a secret: 'Le secret douloureux des Dieux et des rois: c'est que les hommes sont libres. Ils sont libres, Egisthe. Tu le sais, et ils ne le savent pas' (*M*, p. 77). This is precisely the source of Egisthe's weariness, since he is aware that he must exert himself without respite in order to hide from other men the fact of their liberty—and the first victim of his mesmeric dance is himself. 'Dieu tout-puissant, qui suis-je, sinon la peur que les autres ont de moi?', he asks Jupiter (*M*, p. 78). What, indeed? But at least the fear people have of him is based in part upon the fact that he effectively exercises the power of life and death over people. His mistake is to believe Jupiter as all-powerful as people suppose, and he wonders why Jupiter himself does not deal with Oreste:

Egisthe: (. . .) Dieu tout-puissant, qu'attends-tu pour le foudroyer?
Jupiter, lentement: Pour le foudroyer? (*Un temps. Las et voûté.*) Egisthe, les Dieux ont un autre secret . . .
Egisthe: Que vas-tu me dire?
Jupiter: Quand une fois la liberté a explosé dans une âme d'homme, les Dieux ne peuvent plus rien contre cet homme-là. Car c'est une affaire d'hommes, et c'est aux autres hommes—à eux seuls—qu'il appartient de le laisser courir ou de l'étrangler.

God is powerful only as long as men believe in him. Amongst other things, liberty means liberation—not merely from those procedures which we are too ready to employ to mask from ourselves the need to live a life which does not depend upon stereotyped forms of behaviour, but liberation also from that authority which is imposed upon us by those who wish to see us live in a manner ordered by them. Jupiter is therefore wrong to say to Egisthe: 'Nous faisons tous les deux régner l'ordre'. He himself does not have the power to maintain the reign of anything at all; only Egisthe can act in the real world, and for him it is too late.

When he finds himself confronted with Oreste, Egisthe refuses to defend himself—partly, no doubt, on account of the weariness of which he had complained to Jupiter. But also, as he shows in his remark 'Je veux que tu m'assassines' (*M*, p. 80), because it can serve his purposes to be assassinated rather than killed in a fight. Ever since the death of Agamemnon, Egisthe has had to play the part of a tyrant without, as far as one can see, ever having fully believed in himself as a tyrant. Only real tyrants are assassinated, however; therefore, if Egisthe dies by an assassin's hand, it will be proof that he is a real tyrant. The opportunity is one not to be missed in that it enables him to die having chosen for himself the essence which will define him and to avoid some definition which escapes from his control. The procedure is one of *mauvaise foi*, similar to that of the solid citizens portrayed in the paintings of the museum in Bouville, in that it involves the attempt to be seen by one-self and by others in terms of an image chosen and projected by oneself. That he is not the only character in the play to fall into a state of *mauvaise foi* is illustrated by Electre. Already, at an earlier stage of the play, she had reproached Oreste with making her forget her hatred, her only treasure. Now, seeing Egisthe, the object of her hatred, lying dead before her, she realises that her hatred has died with him. Not only that: given that this hatred was what gave meaning to her life, it follows that its disappearance must result in her life becoming meaningless. Her problem will be that of trying to fill the gap of which she has become aware.

Two ways are open to her; one is the way of authentic action, but it is the more difficult, since it implies accepting the fact of our own con-tingency, as it was observed by Roquentin, and embarking upon a life in which nothing is guaranteed in advance, but in which we have, as it were, to 'reinvent' ourself with each new day. Electre opts for the easier solution, the solution of *mauvaise foi*. Her reaction is after all not sur-prising: for the past fifteen years, she has been shielded from the problem by not being obliged to take on responsibility for her own existence—her hatred was not only her justification, but also a phenomenon she supposed to be temporary. Once her father's assassins were disposed of she would be able to 'live'; now that they *are* dead she seeks a new shield from the reality of life. The explanation is suggested by Electre herself when Oreste invites her to confirm that she wished the death of the regicides, and she replies: 'Je ne sais plus. J'ai rêvé ce crime' (*M*, p. 91). Dreams are not reality; ever since her father's death, Electre had *imagined* the return of Oreste, imagined the death of Egisthe and Clytemnestre, imagined her liberation and her subsequent joy. When imaginary vengeance is suddenly converted into real vengeance it becomes some-thing unrelated to her, since she is incapable of turning her back on the imaginary world and accepting life in the world of reality. 'Voleur!', she says to Oreste, 'Je n'avais presque rien à moi qu'un peu de calme et quelques rêves. Tu m'as tout pris, tu as volé une pauvresse' (M, p. 103). Consequently, she is in a condition to accept the persuasion of Jupiter, who suggests that she did not want the death of Agamemnon's assassins at all: she was young and alone, and had merely played a game suitable to a lonely young girl. All can be put right if she will repent. If she accepts the view God has of her and accepts to behave in a way appropriate to that image, it will be possible for Jupiter to save her from the consequences of the evil action she became involved in despite herself. She accepts the invitation to abandon herself to *mauvaise foi*: instead of following Oreste's suggestion that she should set off with him in search of a true self, she turns to Jupiter and the ready-made portrait of herself that he has painted. 'Au secours!', she cries to Jupiter, 'Défends-moi contre les mouches, contre mon frère, contre moi-même, ne me laisse pas seule, je consacrerai ma vie entière à l'expiation. Je me repens, Jupiter, je me repens' (M, p. 104). Expiation and repentance are appropriate only in a person who accepts that he or she has committed a crime. If this is so, Electre's remorse must put her in a situation similar to that in which her mother had found herself, and it becomes difficult to believe either that Jupiter will defend her against the flies, or that the Furies, at the end of the play, are right to follow Oreste: he, after all, does not accept that the assassination of Egisthe and Clytemnestre is a crime.

But is it true that Oreste himself will now embark on the search for his true self? After the assassination of Egisthe and Clytemnestre, he gives the impression that he is heading in the right direction. When he asserts that his killing of Egisthe is an act of justice which will restore to the people of Argos 'le sentiment de leur dignité' (M, p. 80), he seems to be putting his sword at the service of his fellow-men. Similarly when he talks about his liberty in association with the liberation of the inhabitants of Argos. We are tempted, however, to begin suspecting his motives when he says: 'J'ai fait *mon* acte, Electre, et cet acte était bon. (. . .) Et plus il sera lourd à porter, plus je me réjouirai, car ma liberté, c'est lui' (M, p. 84). At this stage, it already looks as though he is going beyond the idea that his act is the *expression* of his liberty to the notion that it will henceforth be the *justification* of his existence. It is true that, during the confrontation with Jupiter, in which the god attempts to lead him back to right-thinking ways, he gives the right answers; but it is also true that Jupiter's position is so feeble as to make it easy for Oreste to find the appropriate responses. In the first place, Jupiter makes the mistake of speaking about the guilt of an Oreste who claims that the assassination was an act of justice. Secondly, he offers to install Oreste and Electre on the thrones left vacant by Egisthe and Clytemnestre: for one thing, it is evident that such a matter does not depend on him; for another, Oreste knows full well that, by the fact of his birth, the throne is his for the taking; what is more, Jupiter wants to 'give' the throne to the young pair on the same terms as had applied in the case of Egisthe—and Oreste must know, thanks to his having overheard the discussion between Jupiter and Egisthe, that the bargain between them was in any case the result of a confidence trick on the part of the god. Furthermore, as one might expect, given what has already happened, Jupiter has no hope of succeeding in converting Oreste by the big speech intended to overawe him. 'Oreste! Je t'ai créé et j'ai créé toute chose', he begins (M, p. 98), and goes on to prove as best he can that, since man is part of nature and nature follows a series of fixed laws, then Oreste, as a man, should accept to follow those laws, which are, of course, laid down by Jupiter himself. In this speech he understandably omits the point he had earlier made to Egisthe: 'Quand une fois la liberté a explosé dans une âme d'homme, les Dieux ne peuvent plus rien contre cet homme-là' (M, p. 79). Men, in other words, are not simply a part of a well-ordered nature under Jupiter's control, and Oreste is well aware of it: 'Tu es le roi des Dieux, Jupiter, le roi des pierres et des étoiles, le roi des vagues de la mer. Mais tu n'es pas le roi des hommes' (M, p. 99).

Man is free—free in relation to the gods, but also free in a more fundamental way. 'Je suis ma liberté!' (M, p. 100), says Oreste. Formerly, he had not been conscious of the fact. He had accepted the idea that he was part of the natural order of things and subject to the laws of the universe. In human terms, this had meant that he was relieved of a good deal of responsibility for his own activities: 'tu étais mon excuse d'exister', he says to Jupiter, 'car tu m'avais mis au monde pour servir tes desseins, et le monde était une vieille entremetteuse qui me parlait de toi, sans cesse' (M, p. 100). If, therefore, he followed the natural order of things, he could not go astray. But as soon as he perceived that he was in reality a free being, he became totally aware of himself as responsible for his own actions. Now, instead of existing within the reassuring frame-work of a fully organised structure, he finds that he is radically separate from all that surrounds him, and has no alternative but to accept responsibility for his every act: 'je suis condamné à n'avoir d'autre loi que la mienne. (. . .) Car je suis un homme, Jupiter, et chaque homme doit inventer son chemin' (*M*, p. 101).

All this is impeccable within the Sartrean context, and remains so as long as Oreste is contesting the view which Jupiter wishes to impose upon him. Once his independence of Jupiter is established, however, his stance is less obviously authentic. This emerges in his attitude to the people of Argos. The belief that he is in a superior position to them emerges in an unmistakable manner when he says: 'Les hommes d'Argos sont mes hommes. Il faut que je leur ouvre les yeux' (*M*, p. 102). A remark of this kind carries with it the implication that he should work together with *his* people to establish a good form of society in Argos. And yet, when asked by Jupiter what he considers the people of Argos should do with the despair he is about to reveal to them, he makes clear that he does not consider himself involved in their problems. In reply to Jupiter, he affirms that the people must do what they like with their despair: 'ils sont libres, et la vie humaine commence de l'autre côté du désespoir' (*M*, p. 102).[1] Oreste, in fact, is radically egocentric, concerned with his own salvation, rather than with the interests of the people around him. The assassination of Egisthe and Clytemnestre is an expression of his liberty; therefore he is free; consequently he must use his freedom as a means of setting off in search of his true self. This is the idea that he tries to communicate to Electre: 'Nous étions trop légers, Electre: à présent nos pieds s'enfoncent dans la terre comme les roues d'un char dans une ornière. Viens, nous allons partir et nous marcherons à pas lourds, courbés sous notre précieux fardeau' (*M*, p. 104). It is already obvious that the burden has begun to take on some absolute value: it is what will justify Oreste's existence, and is in this respect in no way superior to any other means of providing oneself with a fixed essence. The crime by which Oreste asserted his freedom has already become a defence against the need constantly to accept the implications of a radical freedom, with all that it imposes in the way of a constant obligation to 'reinvent' oneself through each individual action.

Once this is realised, the final scene takes on its full significance. Faced with the hostile crowd, Oreste imposes himself upon them as king: 'Vous voilà donc, mes sujets très fidèles? Je suis Oreste, votre roi', etc. (*M*, p. 107). He is at pains, however, to establish that he is not cast in

[1] We should perhaps note that in this context the word *despair* denotes a lack of reliance on hope (which often leads to an absence of positive action in the world) rather than the idea that life is not worth living, etc.

the same mould as Egisthe—or indeed as Electre in her present situation:
'vous avez lu dans ses yeux', he says of Egisthe, 'qu'il était des vôtres et
qu'il n'avait pas le courage de ses actes' (M, p. 108). Oreste is here admit-
ting by implication that he does not identify himself with the people of
Argos. A practical consequence is that, instead of following Egisthe's
example and using his crime as a link (no matter how painful) between
himself and his subjects, he will take it over completely and employ it
for his own purposes. We cannot believe him when he says that he loves
the people of Argos and killed for them, any more than we can accept
his assertion that he belongs amongst them and is linked to them by
blood: there is too much evidence on the other side. The claim that he
merits the throne already contains within it the suggestion that winning
it was bound up above all with his personal interests; and the point is
made clear when he says: 'Je veux être un roi sans terre et sans sujets'
(M, p. 108). In the interview with Jacques-Alain Miller, already referred
to, Sartre accepts the idea that 'Oreste joue la belle âme', and says,
speaking of the characters in all his plays: 'Le seul héros positif est Goetz
("Le Diable et le bon Dieu"), parce qu'il rentre dans le monde pour y
aider de sa propre expérience, de ce qu'il a compris'. There is no doubt
that, in this respect, Goetz and Oreste are at opposite poles. Goetz accepts
to commit a crime because he realises that it is unavoidable if he is to
undertake action in common with his fellow-men. Oreste's crime is a
justification of his own individual existence: 'vous avez compris que
mon crime est bien à moi; (. . .) il est ma raison de vivre et mon orgueil'
(M, p. 108). Far from remaining in Argos in order, through work undertaken in common to create a society which would have a meaning for all
its inhabitants, Oreste is concerned only to deprive the people of what
had given meaning to their life: 'tout est à moi, je prends tout sur moi'.
It is, of course, true that this *tout* includes crime, remorse, and all the
fears involved in the life of the city, but that is of little importance within
the context; the essential point is that Oreste is concerned to dispossess
the people of what justified their existence because he wants to make use
of it to justify his own.

The whole of his long final speech is directed towards this end. When
he departs, with the Furies hot on his heels, he leaves behind an Argos
in which life does indeed have to be started afresh. One can therefore say
that, from a political point of view, Oreste is a failure. Unlike Roquentin,
but in step with the evolution of Sartre himself, he sees the importance of
the total human and social context as the field of action for the individual.

Does he, however, act in any true sense of the word? During the interview with Jacques-Alain Miller, Sartre explains: 'Un acte devient geste lorsqu'il est en lui-même frappé d'inefficacité'. The most obvious way in which this can happen is when something we do fails to produce the expected results because of the intervention of some other person (for example, Frantz, in *Les Séquestrés d'Altona*, saves a Rabbi from the Nazis in the full knowledge that his action will be severely punished. His father, by using his influence with the authorities, saves Frantz from punishment—and so his act is reduced to the status of a gesture). It is nevertheless equally possible to reduce our own acts to gestures, as Oreste himself demonstrates. He claims that, by killing Egisthe and Clytemnestre, he has made the people of Argos free. This freedom is what would confer upon the assassination the character of an act. But in order to ensure the continued existence of this all-important freedom, it would be necessary for Oreste to remain in Argos and, through his joint efforts with the people, do all in his power to maintain that freedom. Such is not the case: as we have seen, Electre has already accepted the bargain proposed by Jupiter, and this may well mean that the people of Argos are going to find themselves in much the same position as before the arrival of Oreste—it will be remembered that the bargain included the offer by Jupiter (*M*, pp. 96–7) to put Electre, with Oreste, on the now vacant throne, provided that they repudiated their crime, and it is perhaps reasonable to suppose that the offer still stands. Given this hypothesis, the people of Argos may find that, instead of living under the tyranny of Egisthe and Clytemnestre, they will now live under that of Electre. Oreste's 'act', in other words, if it is deprived of the consequences which should have followed it, will turn out to be no more than a gesture, but a gesture upon which he will base an attitude of *mauvaise foi*, since he looks to it for a permanent definition of himself ('il est ma raison de vivre et mon orgueil'). The assassination, transposed thus on to the plane of the myth, takes on the characteristics of the imaginary, and resembles the novel conceived of by Roquentin—or the fantasies indulged in by Sartre the small boy.

But even at this level, Oreste can be assured of nothing. The image of himself which he hopes to leave in the minds of the people of Argos is the one he projects with care in his final speech. If there is some certainty that the image will remain stable in his own consciousness, there is no guarantee that the population of Argos will remain the faithful mirror he would like it to be. He cannot know what the future of the city will be; he should realise that it is at least possible for his 'subjects', in his absence, to interpret the image in a way which would not suit him. Oreste himself, by the meaning he gives to his 'act', seeks to give a meaning to his existence. The people of Argos may prove to have good reason to endow the same facts with a different significance, and in that case, Oreste will have left himself at their mercy.

*   *   *

In a sense, then, it is true that Oreste, though echoing the social and political awareness towards which Sartre moves between *La Nausée* and *Les Mouches*, finishes up in a position which is inferior to that of Roquentin at the point where his diary ends. It is true that Roquentin's final attitude is solipsistic and asocial in the sense that he turns to the work of art, an individual creation, for a solution to the problem presented by his contingent existence. But it is also true that, if his solution is unsatisfactory from a social point of view, it has much to be said for it within its own terms: for Sartre, as we have seen, the work of art (*any* work of art, including *Some of these days*) exists in an absolute way which makes it unassailable, and so permits it to confer an absolute necessity upon its creator. Oreste's weakness is that he attempts to apply Roquentin's solution to a non-absolute situation. In *Les Mouches*, the equivalent of Roquentin's novel is Oreste's final speech; but the word 'equivalent' should not be taken to mean 'equal', because there is a vital difference between the novel and the speech. One may undoubtedly conceive of both in terms of the imaginary; it is possible, for example, to say that by his final speech and his immediate departure from Argos, Oreste seeks to transform *himself* into a myth—and a myth is, of course, a product of the imagination. One thing certain is that Oreste, perhaps as a result of the divorce from reality of which he complained at the beginning of the play, never descends from the realm of the ideal. This is not true of Roquentin; his novel, if he writes it, will indeed be an ideal creation, but it will of necessity exist outside him, and it is for this reason that it may be effective as a guarantee of his own necessary existence. Oreste's mistake is to want, as it were, *himself to be the novel*. He hopes to turn his assassination of Egisthe and Clytemnestre into a kind of adventure which will give him a place in Argos without any reference to the reality which is Argos. But a place in a human community can only be earned gradually by real action carried out day by day in a real world along with real men. Oreste seeks to make use of men in order to achieve the impossible ambition of making an *ideal* place in a *real* society.

In *Les Mots*, Sartre speaks of the way in which, as a boy, he imagined stories where frail young girls were precipitated by him into such perilous situations that he alone was capable of saving them. He goes on:

> Quand les janissaires brandissaient leurs cimeterres courbes, un gémissement parcourait le désert et les rochers disaient au sable: "Il y a quelqu'un qui manque ici: c'est Sartre." A l'instant, j'écartais le paravent, je faisais voler les têtes à coups de sabre, je naissais dans un fleuve de sang. Bonheur d'acier! J'étais à ma place.
>
> (*Mo*, p. 93)

The process is precisely the one followed by Oreste: he too believes that he gives birth to himself in a river of blood. In *Les Mots*, of course, Sartre is speaking of his childhood self, long before the period between 1938 and 1943, when he became politically and socially conscious and understood that action in the world can only be action among men. *Les Mouches* is without doubt a reflection of this evolution, even if only as an expression of the fact that the period of the war saw Sartre begin to write plays, which must, in one way or another, deal with relationships between people. Oreste serves to underline the difficulty of authentic action in a human context, and is merely the first in a series of characters who will fail to overcome that difficulty. Earlier, we quoted Sartre to the effect that Goetz is his only positive hero, since he is the only one to put his experiences at the service of the society around him, without seeking to occupy a favoured position in that society. Goetz appears in *Le Diable et le bon Dieu*, produced in 1951, at a time when Sartre himself had at last begun to understand that the attempt to achieve some sort of absolute Salvation is not a worthwhile project; Oreste and *Les Mouches* clearly represent a very early step in the movement which will lead to that realisation.

Conclusion

We started off by saying that the aim of this book would be to study *La Nausée* and *Les Mouches* with a view to throwing light on the early stages of Sartre's evolution. The analysis of the two texts shows that it is indeed a matter of early stages in an evolution: when seen in terms of Sartre's ideas on the imaginary and of his autobiography, *Les Mots*, the movement from the solitary Roquentin to the Oreste who realises the importance of other people is more apparent than real. The explanation is not hard to find: in *Les Mots*, the self-portrait put before us shows a Sartre who not only turned to writing as a means of salvation in his early years but also continued until middle-age to look to literature as a way of justifying his existence. We are not, of course, bound to accept at its face value everything we read in an autobiography, since authors sometimes use this form of writing as a method by which they can persuade their public to accept a distorted image of themselves. In the case of Sartre, however, the evidence of *Les Mots* confirms what can be deduced from the rest of his work.

At the beginning of the chapter on *Les Mouches*, we quoted Sartre's view that the theatre ought to be 'a great collective religious phenomenon', and underlined the word 'collective' as indicating an evolution towards action undertaken in common with other men. It is important to note, however, that in the same phrase Sartre talks of the theatre as a *religious* phenomenon; and it is certain that a theatrical representation shares with religious acts undertaken in common a formal, ritualistic character which is of some importance. This is not the place to discuss Sartre's attitude to religion in general; the point we should note is that, through a large part of his career, the way in which he conceives of the theatre is not so very different from his view of the novel. A sentence from *Les Mots*, quoted earlier, provides the link: 'J'étais à la Messe: j'assistais à l'éternel retour des noms et des événements' (*Mo*, p. 36). The reference is specifically to the stories read to Sartre by his mother, but could equally well describe the 'great collective religious phenomenon' of the theatre. One could even go so far as to suggest that, for a man seeking through literature some proof that his existence is necessary, the theatre is a more satisfactory medium than the novel. If Roquentin produces the novel about which he speaks in the closing pages of *La Nausée*, his existence may indeed be justified by the work of art produced by him, but only in a relatively abstract manner: he is, after all, seeking 'salvation' by a means which in no way depends on other people because, even if no one ever reads his novel, even if it is never published, its existence will be no less necessary and no less absolute. A play, as a piece of literature, is similar in this respect to a novel; the big difference between the two is that, when a play is performed, both the actors and the public collaborate in the production of the total theatrical pheno-menon. In a sense, both groups put themselves at the service of the author: if, as we suggested in the Introduction, we can begin to 'see' Hamlet only when we cease to see Laurence Olivier, the implication is that Olivier accepts to 'disappear' so that Hamlet may make his appear-ance. There can be no doubt that Sartre is aware of the way in which the actor is an analogon and must be prepared to abdicate his identity in order that the character may be evoked. In the first place, we have the evidence provided in *L'Imaginaire*; in addition, we learn during the course of *La Nausée* that Anny thought she would be able to realise perfect moments in the theatre—only to discover that, as an actress, she could be no more than a means by which perfect moments might be realised for others (*N*, p. 191); and later on, in his adaptation of Dumas's *Kean*, Sartre will show an actor who is threatened by complete loss of identity through the fact of having to make himself subservient to the roles he plays. As for the public which goes to see the play, the individuals which make it up can perceive that work of art, a product of its author's imagination, only by transposing themselves on to the plane of the imaginary: in this respect, they are like the audience which goes to hear Beethoven's Seventh Symphony. The actors and the public therefore make up a group of real people who come together specific-ally so that the product of the author's imagination shall exist, and for that very reason confirm the reality of the author who produced the work.

From this, we can conclude that Sartre is at the same time like Roquen-tin and different from him. They are similar in that, as we have shown, both look to the work of art as a means of conferring upon their own existence a necessity it otherwise lacks. One of the differences between them is that, by the end of *La Nausée*, Roquentin has not produced his novel, whereas Sartre, over a long period of years, has produced a series of works of the imagination. Like Roquentin, Sartre the author of creative literature looked first to the novel (at any rate if one is to judge by his published work); in other words, he sought, as an answer to the problem of his own contingency, the solution one might have expected from the author of *L'Imaginaire*: Roquentin's adventure, as described by Sartre, shows how his ideas about the imaginary can be exploited with a view to justifying one's existence without reference to other men. The Sartre who, as a boy, considered that his reality was denied by those around him, discovers a way of asserting his reality that owes nothing to anyone but himself.

When, in due course, he turns to the theatre, his project is not so very different. Although, as we have suggested, the actors and the public put themselves at his service in the sense of confirming his existence by recognising the existence of the play created by him, this is in fact merely the novelist's project carried one stage further: a play, like a novel, is a work of art, and both, in the Sartrean context, fulfil the same function. But the difference between Roquentin, who, as it were, opts out of the human context, and Oreste, who aspires to action within a human situation, is nevertheless an important one. Earlier, we quoted the passage in Simone de Beauvoir's *La Force de l'âge* which says that by February 1940 Sartre had come to the conclusion that men should 'assume their situation': *Les Mouches* is the first of a series of plays which will show us characters trying to do precisely that. Sartre, at this stage, has realised that we shall find no solution to the problem of our contingency by turning our back on the real world peopled by other men. The trouble is, and will continue to be, that acting within a human situation presents its special problems, and these problems are none other than the ones which, according to *Les Mots*, led Sartre to seek justification through the work of art: since we can never really be sure that other people see us as we believe ourselves to be, the temptation is for us to behave in such a way that those around us will accept an image which we choose to project. In other words, instead of accepting the uncertainty that must result from our existence amongst other men, we have recourse to procedures of *mauvaise foi*, and try to define our essence once and for all. The result is that Sartre's plays are largely concerned with a series of characters who try, and fail, to come to terms with their human situation. This, as we tried to show, is true of Oreste; one can say that, through his desire to transform himself into a myth, he wants not only to *be* the work of art, but also the author of that work of art. His *mauvaise foi* consists in trying, through the real world of men, to exist in an unreal world which escapes the influence of the real.

It follows that, if Sartre himself can be compared to Roquentin, we should not assume that he can also be compared directly to Oreste. It is true that, according to his own account of his boyhood, Sartre often made himself the hero of his own imaginary stories, but the stories were imagined in solitude and did not involve other real people. In a sense, therefore, we can say that, when he comes to write plays, he avoids the pitfalls of his own characters: by producing characters who are in a state of *mauvaise foi*, he does not himself fall into a state of *mauvaise foi*, since in his plays, as in his novels, it might be held that his reference is less to other people than to some absolute. But Sartre himself would not claim to be completely blameless; like Roquentin, he wished to be cleansed of the sin of existence and to achieve salvation through writing. By the time he comes to *Les Mots*, he realises the futility of such an ambition, and asks: 'Si je range l'impossible Salut au magasin des accessoires, que reste-t-il? Tout un homme, fait de tous les hommes et qui les vaut et que vaut n'importe qui' (*Mo*, p. 213). The realisation is an important one in that it involves accepting the idea that a writer has no special prestige. Hitherto, Sartre had resembled both his own grandfather, and the Goetz of the earlier part of *Le Diable et le bon Dieu*. Of the first, he says: 'Charles Schweitzer était trop comédien pour n'avoir pas besoin d'un Grand Spectateur' (*Mo*, p. 80): his point of reference is a God, in whom he does not really believe. Similarly with Goetz—rejected by men because of his illegitimate birth, he decides first of all that he will be Evil, on the grounds that he will thus oblige God (the absolute) to take notice of him. When it is suggested that everyone is in any case evil, he undertakes to realise the Good, again in order that he may impose himself upon the attention of God. Only when he realises that both projects were abortive does he accept the idea that life is something which should simply be lived, without reference to any absolute, and that this means accepting action in collaboration with other men. Sartre himself reaches the same realisation; but the question of whether he comes to as satisfactory a conclusion as Goetz is one which takes us a good deal beyond the evidence to be found in *La Nausée* and *Les Mouches*.

Bibliographical Note

A very large number of books and articles have been devoted to Sartre; their value varies a great deal. I shall therefore mention here only a few titles which may be found useful by those who would like to extend their reading and to set the preceding pages against a wider background.

Francis Jeanson's *Sartre par lui-même* (published by the Editions du Seuil in their series 'Ecrivains de toujours') first appeared in 1955, and concentrates mainly on Sartre's theatre. It has recently been revised to take account of later work. The great merit of the book is that, although Jeanson identifies himself closely with Sartre's work, the analyses he gives are nevertheless very penetrating and reveal with a great deal of success the continuity of certain preoccupations to be found in Sartre's theatre. Anthony Manser, *Sartre, a philosophic study* (London, The Athlone Press, 1966) is a sympathetic account by an English philosopher. Its weakest chapters are perhaps those on the novels and the plays; otherwise, it provides a clear and helpful exposition of Sartre's thought. Iris Murdoch, *Sartre, romantic rationalist* ('Studies in Modern European Literature and Thought', Cambridge, Bowes and Bowes, 1953), contains, among other things, a very good analysis of *La Nausée*; it remains valuable, even though Miss Murdoch was inevitably limited to Sartre's production in the period up to 1953. Rhiannon Goldthorpe has written two articles specifically on *La Nausée* and its relationship with Sartre's philosophy; the first, 'The Presentation of consciousness in Sartre's *La Nausée* and its theoretical basis: Reflection and facticity', appeared in *French Studies* (XXII, 2, pp. 114–32) in April 1968; the second, 'Transcendence and intentionality', in *French Studies* (XXV, 1, pp. 32–46) in January 1971.[1] An account of Sartre's work as a playwright will be found in my own article (referred to earlier): 'The Theatre of Sartre: 1940–1965' (*Books Abroad*, vol. 41, no 2, Spring 1967, pp. 133–49).

---

[1] I should like to express my gratitude to Mrs Goldthorpe for having read the present study in manuscript, and for having made many valuable comments and criticisms.

M. Adereth's book, *Commitment in modern French literature* (London, Gollancz, 1967), includes a useful fifty-page section on Sartre, as well as a more general discussion of the question of *engagement*.

As for Sartre's own writing, two books in which he gives an account of himself are also of direct interest for the light they throw upon his work, and upon his evolution during the years which saw the publication of *La Nausée* and *Les Mouches*. The first of them, *Les Mots* (Paris, Gallimard, 1964), has been drawn upon in the course of this study. The second, *Sartre*[1] (Paris, Gallimard, 1977) is the transcript of the film *Sartre par lui-même* (shot in 1972, but issued only in 1976), in which Sartre discusses with some of his closest associates the political and intellectual development which has led him away from many of the attitudes to be found in his writing of the 30s and 40s.

Finally, a work which cannot be too highly recommended is Michel Contat and Michel Rybalka, *Les Ecrits de Sartre* (Paris, Gallimard, 1970), well described by its sub-title: 'Chronologie, bibliographie commentée'. The value of this book lies not only in its mass of biographical and bibliographical detail, but also in its summaries and in the explanations of the circumstances surrounding Sartre's different publications, as well as in the Appendix, which reproduces many texts not easily found elsewhere.

[1] *Sarte*, un film réalisé par Alexandre Astruc et Michel Contat, avec la participation de Simone de Beauvoir, Jacques-Laurent Bost, André Gorz, Jean Pouillon. Texte intégral.